Sir Ivor 1968

Crepello 1957

Roberto 1972

The Minstrel 1977
(Jubilee year.)

Eighth Epsom Derby - 1977

Peter Biegel
'77

LESTER'S
DERBYS

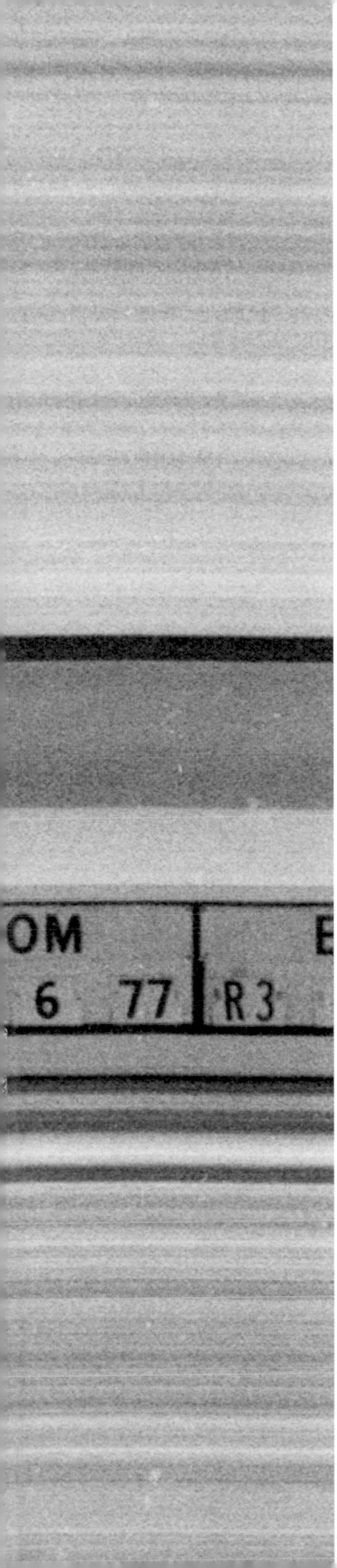

LESTER'S DERBYS

LESTER PIGGOTT

and

SEAN MAGEE

methuen

First published in Great Britain 2004 by
Methuen Publishing Limited
215 Vauxhall Bridge Road
London SW1V 1EJ

1 3 5 7 9 10 8 6 4 2

A CIP catalogue record for this book is available from the British Library.

ISBN 0 413 77411 2

Printed and bound in Great Britain by the Bath Press.

Endpapers:
*Peter Biegel's painting of Lester Piggott's first eight Derby winners, 1977.
In his book* Peter Biegel's Racing Pictures *(1983) the artist notes that
'I find it very difficult to keep up with Mr Piggott's Classic wins!'*

Half-title:
*Empery and Lester return after winning the 1976 Derby. (For the full-size
version, see pages 146–7.)*

Title spread:
*The official photofinish print of the 1977 Derby: The Minstrel wins by a
neck from Hot Grove.*

Contents

'The Thoroughbred exists because its selection has depended not on experts, technicians or zoologists, but on a piece of wood: the winning post of the Epsom Derby.'

Federico Tesio

Preface

When Lester Piggott won his ninth Derby on Teenoso in June 1983, Tony Morris – then as now one of the most informed and articulate racing writers – saw no reason to underplay the status of the hero of the hour. Lester was 'the supreme artist plying his craft from the saddle, his genius as sublime as that of a Rembrandt or a Beethoven, and his accomplishments on the same plane. In the sporting world there has been nobody to match him in his lifetime … George Best bestrode his sphere like a Colossus for a season, Gary Sobers for perhaps five, but for the best part of three decades – truly the best part of us who know – Lester has been the pre-eminent leader of his field.' Over twenty years later, in December 2003, Will Buckley in the *Observer* picked up the same theme: 'There are very few British sportsmen over the past fifty years who could claim to have been arguably the best in the world in their fields for a decade (Daley Thompson, yes; Nick Faldo, perhaps, Ian Botham, maybe). Piggott is the only one who could argue that he was probably the best in the world for three decades.'

Except, of course, that Lester would argue no such thing. For the one person guaranteed to take a matter-of-fact attitude towards his extraordinary career – riding winners in six consecutive decades from the 1940s to the 1990s, with his 4,493 winners in Britain including a record nine Derby winners from thirty-six rides, thirty Classics in all, etc. etc. – is the man himself. For him 'a race is a race', be it the Derby or a selling plate at Folkestone. Or, as John Oaksey put it after Empery had brought the record-setting seventh Derby victory, 'The icy confidence which has always been one of Lester's most priceless qualities has the effect, at Epsom on Derby Day, of turning what is, for other men, a complex and nerve-wracking occasion into an ordinary job of work.'

It is highly unlikely that Lester Piggott's record in the Derby, still the most famous Flat race in the world, will ever be equalled, and the simple aim of this book is to celebrate that record with a book published on the fiftieth anniversary of his first Derby winner, Never Say Die in 1954.

The text of the book is divided into two 'voices':

The introductory and linking passages set in
this type are by myself.

Text set in this type gives Lester's own
account of the nine Derby winners
– and some of the losers.

For Lester, winning nine Derbys may have been 'an ordinary job of work'. For me, it is one of the most remarkable records in all sport. We both hope you enjoy the book.

Sean Magee
April 2004

Acknowledgements

Apart from Lester himself, who once he had been persuaded out of his initial diffidence about the project has been unstinting in his time and assistance, three people have performed a signal service to the publication of this book. The first is Lester's wife Susan, who gave me free run of the scrapbooks, documents and photographs accumulated over a riding career which spanned nearly half a century, and dispensed considerable hospitality while doing so. The second is Sir Peter O'Sullevan, whose own record books proved an invaluable source, and whose recollections of the fifty-year friendship between journalist and jockey offered many insights into Lester's character. And the third is John Schwartz at Methuen, whose design and typesetting skills were put to a quite unreasonable test by a complicated book delivered not exactly on time, and emerged triumphant. Thanks also to Stephen Wallis at Epsom Downs, John Randall at the *Racing Post*, Peter Bell, and Geoff Greetham at Timeform, Chris Pitt, Tim Cox, Willie Newton, Jeremy Richardson, George Bailey and Katie Donovan – and a special vote of thanks to The Three Musketeers of racecourse photography, Gerry Cranham, Ed Byrne and George Selwyn.

Many of the illustrations in this book come from Lester's own collection, and it has not always been possible to track down the copyright holders. Any omissions of the correct copyright notice will of course be rectified in future editions if the publishers Methuen are notified. Sources of other illustrations are as follows: Anne Hall: endpapers; Gerry Cranham: half title, vi, 66–7, 118, 144, 146–7, 155, 156, 158, 164–5, 171, 175, 178, 190–1, 195, 200, 204, 207, 210–11; RaceTech: title spread, 124–5; Press Association: 3, 46–7, 85; *Daily Mail*: 6–7; Hulton-Getty: x–1, 11, 34–5, 61, 86, 112; Baron: 22; *Daily Express*: 43, 133; David Cunningham: 84; Dell Hancock: 98; the *Sun*: 109; Sotheby's: 113; Mirrorpix: 114–15, 135, 179; Sean Magee: 122; Central Press: 131; Provincial Press Agency: 154; George Selwyn: 173–4, 214–15, 220, 223; Sport and General: 180–1; Ed Byrne: 219.

S.M.

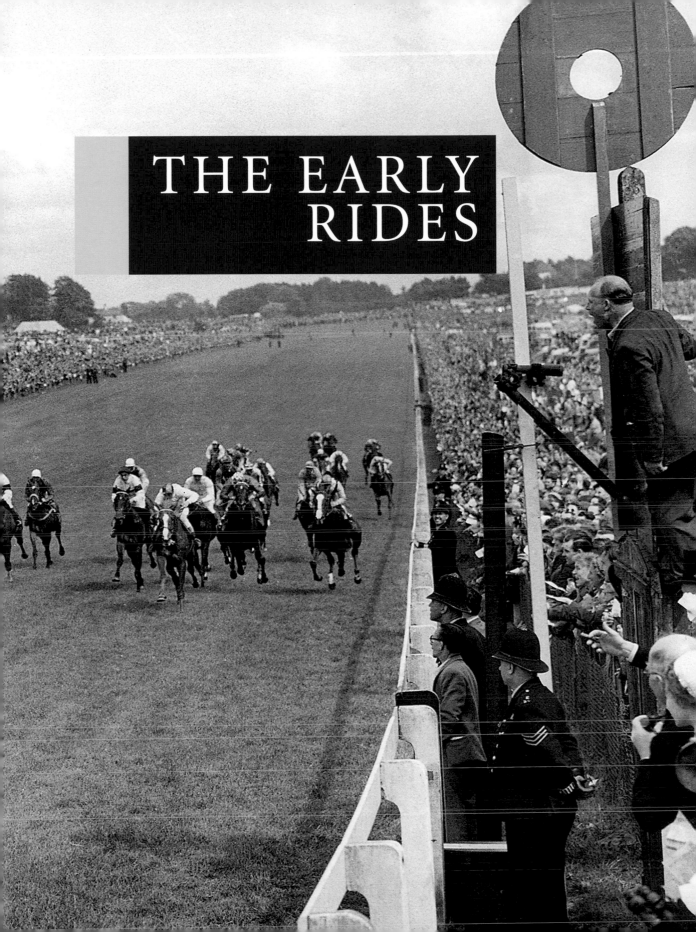

THE EARLY RIDES

The Derby is in Lester Piggott's blood. On his father's side he traces back to the Day family of Danebury, a fabled racing dynasty whose members included Sam Day, who rode the Derby winner three times: Gustavus in 1821, Priam in 1830 and Pyrrhus the First (trained by his brother John) in 1846. Lester's great-great-grandfather Tom Cannon won on the filly Shotover in 1882, and Tom's sons (Lester's great-uncles) Morny and Kempton Cannon each rode one Derby winner – on Flying Fox (1899) and St Amant (1904) respectively. Their sister Margaret was Lester's grandmother.

On his mother's side Lester's ancestors include his great-great-grandfather Fred Rickaby, who trained the 1855 Derby winner Wild Dayrell. (The Piggotts also have a strong connection with National Hunt racing. Lester's grandfather Ernest Piggott rode the Grand National winner three times – Jerry M in 1912 and Poethlyn in 1918 and 1919 – and his father Keith won the Champion Hurdle on African Sister in 1939 and trained 1963 Grand National winner Ayala.)

Born in Wantage, near Newbury, on 5 November 1935, Lester was always destined to be a jockey. Apprenticed to his father's yard at Lambourn, he had his first ride in public on The Chase at Salisbury in April 1948. Later that season the same filly provided him with his first winner, in the Wigan Lane Selling Handicap at Haydock Park on 18 August 1948. He was twelve years old.

It was over a year before he rode his second winner, but by 1950 he was clearly a young jockey of quite exceptional talent, and the major stables were starting to engage him. In September 1950 he won his first big race, the Jockey Club Stakes at Newmarket on Holmbush, trained by Arthur Budgett, and that season he was champion apprentice for the first time with 52 winners, and finished eleventh overall in the jockeys' table.

Lester's first ride in the Derby came in 1951 in the 172nd running of a race first staged in 1780. The Derby is not the oldest Classic race – that distinction belongs to the St Leger, first run in 1776, while the Oaks, first run in 1779, is also older – but it is by a considerable margin the most famous Flat race in the world and has spawned a host of imitators around the globe (many of which Lester has himself won: see pages 233–4).

Racing tradition has it that the Derby was born at a celebration dinner after the first running of the Oaks, a new race for three-year-old fillies on

Epsom Downs, in May 1779. The 12th Earl of Derby – after whose house near Epsom the fillies' race was named – and his aristocratic friends were so pleased with the first Oaks that they decided to stage another new race for three-year-olds the following year, this time to include colts. The Earl, so the story goes (though it cannot be authenticated) tossed a coin with the great Turf administrator Sir Charles Bunbury to decide whose name the new race should bear, and the Earl won. The first Derby was run over one mile on 4 May 1780 and won by Sir Charles's colt Diomed. Four years later in 1784 the distance of the race was increased to one and a half miles, at which it has remained ever since.

Young Lester, aged fifteen in December 1950.

The Derby's status soon grew, helped along by royal patronage: the ninth running, in 1788, went to Sir Thomas, owned by the Prince of Wales, later George IV. (The Prince's Stand, still an Epsom landmark just beyond the winning post, was constructed around this time.) By the early nineteenth century large crowds congregated on the Downs to watch the race, and by the middle of that century Derby Day was firmly established as an unofficial public holiday for Londoners. For many years Parliament suspended business that day so that Members could go to the race, and writers such as Dickens and Trollope saw the Derby Day crowd, ranging from aristocrats in the grandstand to the masses up on the Downs, as a true microcosm of English society.

The status of the occasion was matched by that of the race itself, victory in which soon became the pinnacle of achievement for any three-year-old colt (and very occasionally filly). Practically all the great racehorses of the nineteenth century won the race, and for most of the twentieth century the Derby remained unassailably the greatest Flat race in the world, the one race which every owner, trainer and jockey was desperate to win. Its pre-eminent status was encapsulated in the 1950s by the Italian breeder Federico Tesio, who memorably observed: 'The Thoroughbred exists because its selection has depended not on experts, technicians or zoologists, but on a piece of wood: the winning post of the Epsom Derby.'

Lester Piggott was fifteen years old when he made his first attempt at getting to that piece of wood before his rivals. Unfortunately his partner that day did not share his enthusiasm for the task.

Zucchero was the first really top-class horse I rode, and on his day – though such occasions admittedly could not be predicted with any great accuracy – he remains one of the best I ever sat on. As a two-year-old he was trained initially by Michael Blackmore at Whatcombe (where Paul Cole now trains), and his early career was highly promising. He finished second in his first two races – at Birmingham, and in a valuable race at Sandown Park, where he was beaten half a length. He then won a modest maiden plate at Warwick, and after going on to finish runner-up in the New Stakes at Royal Ascot looked set to develop into one of the leading two-year-olds of the season. But before his next race at Salisbury he showed some of the signs of bad temperament which had blighted the career of his sire Nasrullah. He was unruly at the start (a starting gate in those days, of course, as this was long before the introduction of stalls), planted himself when the tapes went up, and took no part in the race. He repeated these antics in the National Breeders' Produce Stakes at Sandown Park – then one of the most important two-year-old races of the year, and won in 1950 by the subsequent One Thousand Guineas winner Belle Of All – and at the St Leger meeting at Doncaster, and went into winter quarters the winner of just one of his seven races and a source more of exasperation than promise. By then he had moved from Michael Blackmore to Ryan Jarvis, and then on again to Ken Cundell – which is how I came in for the ride.

By early 1951 I was getting plenty of rides from Ken Cundell. He knew that Zucchero had a huge amount of ability but a reluctance to deploy it, and in an effort to find the key to the horse put him in the care of one of his best lads. Initially this appeared not to be working – or at least not to any predictable pattern. When I first rode Zucchero in a race, in the Henry VIII Stakes at Hurst Park – his first outing of 1951 – he played up at the start before eventually deigning to jump off. In the circumstances he ran respectably enough to finish fourth, and followed that performance with an easy victory in the Blue Riband Trial Stakes over an extended mile of the Derby course. Zucchero's behaviour before this race was impeccable, and we began to think that he might be a serious contender for the Derby after all.

Concern over how Zucchero would behave on the day provided a distraction for me from getting too excited about my first ride in the Derby – though to be honest I can't recall having too many butterflies in the stomach – and doubtless also played its part in making his starting price 28–1. Ken Cundell was not a man to take chances, and he did everything he could think of to keep the horse sweet. He instructed me not to carry my whip during the interminable preliminaries to the race (I was given it once we arrived at the starting gate) and took the precaution of himself walking with us over to the start to soothe Zucchero on his way. If the horse got off on equal terms with the others he had a major chance, and any ploy to keep his mind on the job in hand was worth it.

Following pages: Lester's first Derby, 31 May 1951: Zucchero's trainer Ken Cundell vainly points the way.

The starter of the Derby in those days was Major Robinson, and when Ken saw him moving over towards his rostrum he took hold of Zucchero's reins – as gently as he could – and started to lead us in. The starter called us forward, the other runners moved towards the tape, Ken led Zucchero in – and then the horse's mulish side got the better of him again: he dug his toes in, and despite Ken's ever more frantic urgings simply would not move forward. After what felt like an eternity but in fact can only have been a few seconds Zucchero consented to start, and we set off in pursuit of the rest of the runners, who by now were halfway up the hill. But of course it was far too late. Although we eventually caught up with the backmarkers we could never get to grips with the leaders, and finished well behind the winner Arctic Prince.

It was a dismal start to my Derby career, for when at his most cooperative Zucchero would certainly have won that race – as subsequent events were soon to show.

After Epsom, Zucchero won his next three races – ridden by Gordon Richards at Chepstow and by me at Windsor and Sandown Park. Then in July he went to Ascot for the inaugural running of what is now the King George VI and Queen Elizabeth Diamond Stakes, where his rivals included Arctic Prince and both that year's Guineas winners Ki Ming and Belle Of All. I bided my time on Zucchero and did not mount a challenge until halfway up the straight, but after a furious battle we were beaten three quarters of a length by Supreme Court. It was annoying to go so close, but at least the Ascot race showed just how good Zucchero could be when he chose to behave. He was a far better horse than Arctic Prince, who had won his Derby.

Later that season Charlie Spares was aboard when Zucchero was unplaced in the St Leger, as I had been injured in a fall at Lingfield Park the previous month which ruled me out for the rest of the season.

Zucchero was kept in training at four and at five, but his behaviour did not improve with age. Phil Bull, founder of the Timeform organisation, wrote of the five-year-old that 'This brilliant but exasperatingly erratic horse behaved in 1953 like the girl in the nursery rhyme, who when she was good was very very good, but when she was bad she was horrid. He had eight races, and in four of them he simply refused to have anything to do with the game.' The high point of his 1953 campaign came when, two years after the Derby fiasco, he returned to Epsom for the Coronation Cup. Ridden by Lester and starting at 100–7, he won by a length from Wilwyn, who the previous year had won the Washington DC International in the USA. Zucchero's final race was the 1953 Prix de l'Arc de Triomphe at Longchamp: ridden by Lester (his first Arc ride), he set off with the other runners, then after about fifty yards decided that it was not to be one of his going days, and pulled himself up.

Lester's second ride in the Derby in 1952 was on Gay Time, owned by J. V. Rank.

It was late in the 1951 season that I was approached by Jimmy Rank about taking a retainer to ride his horses, and I jumped at the chance. He was one of the very top racehorse owners, and his Flat horses were trained by Noel Cannon at Druid's Lodge on Salisbury Plain, a yard famous as the home of the Druid's Lodge Conspiracy, a group of big gamblers who at the turn of the twentieth century had pulled off some massive betting coups.

Unfortunately Mr Rank died early in 1952 before I had much opportunity to get to know him, and the running of the stable was taken over by his wife Pat. It was declared that the horses would eventually be sold off, but we agreed that I would continue to ride them through the 1952 season.

The most promising Rank three-year-old that spring appeared to be Gay Time, who as a two-year-old had won three races, including the Richmond Stakes at Goodwood and the Solario Stakes at Sandown Park. There were high hopes for the colt at three, but he took a while to come to hand in the spring of 1952 and was distinctly backward when well beaten in the Two Thousand Guineas Trial at Kempton Park and then in the Two Thousand Guineas itself. But with just a week to go before the Derby, he won over a mile and a quarter at Salisbury, and it was decided he would take his chance at Epsom.

Although he started at 25–1 it seemed to me that he could very well win, as there was no outstanding horse in that year's Derby field and Gay Time was clearly improving.

On the day, however, nothing went according to plan. Gay Time managed to tear a shoe off while he was being saddled and had to parade by himself in front of the stands, as by the time the shoe had been replaced the other runners were already halfway across the Downs on the way to the start. There was a very big field of thirty-three runners, and after we were slowly away it proved a struggle to get Gay Time up into a prominent position, which even in those very early days I realised was essential if you had a serious chance in the Derby. He had a very rough passage down the hill, but began to pick up once we had come round Tattenham Corner and straightened up for home. Up the straight he made rapid progress, and with just over a furlong to go only Charlie Smirke on the Aga Khan's Tulyar was ahead of us. Tulyar was on the inside, Gay Time challenging on the outside, and we came very close together, with Gay Time getting the worse of a bumping match and finishing up in the middle of the track. Gay Time was doing his level best to get past Tulyar but we just couldn't wear him down, and at the post we were beaten by three quarters of a length. As we pulled up I was just thinking that I might well get the race on an objection, when Gay Time stumbled at the track which in those days crossed the course soon after the winning post, and deposited me on the ground. He galloped off through the paddock area, and by the time he was caught by a mounted policeman over a mile away in the woods and brought back, the time limit for lodging an objection had expired. A thoroughly frustrating race.

Gay Time then ran in the King George VI and Queen Elizabeth Stakes at Ascot in July, where he again faced Tulyar. We took the lead a furlong out and I thought we'd win, but then Tulyar appeared from out of nowhere and won by a neck – 'very cleverly', according to the form book, and I couldn't argue with that.

I didn't ride Gay Time again, as he was sold to the National Stud and leased to the Queen. Walter Nightingall trained him to win the Gordon Stakes at Goodwood, and he was subsequently moved to Noel

The Derby finish, 1952: Charlie Smirke on Tulyar beats Lester and Gay Time by three quarters of a length.

Murless, in whose charge he was fifth behind Tulyar in the St Leger. He was then retired.

My third Derby ride, in 1953, was Prince Charlemagne, trained at Epsom by Tommy Carey. His starting price of 66–1 just about reflected his chance: he'd shown some decent form as a two-year-old, but come Derby Day was still without a win to his name, and never made any impression on the race, finishing way down the field behind Sir Victor Sassoon's Pinza, ridden by Gordon Richards.

*   *   *

In 1953 Gordon Richards, who retired the following year as the winning-most jockey in British racing history and in all was champion jockey twenty-six times, was winning the Derby for the first time at his twenty-eighth attempt. Lester himself did not have to wait so long.

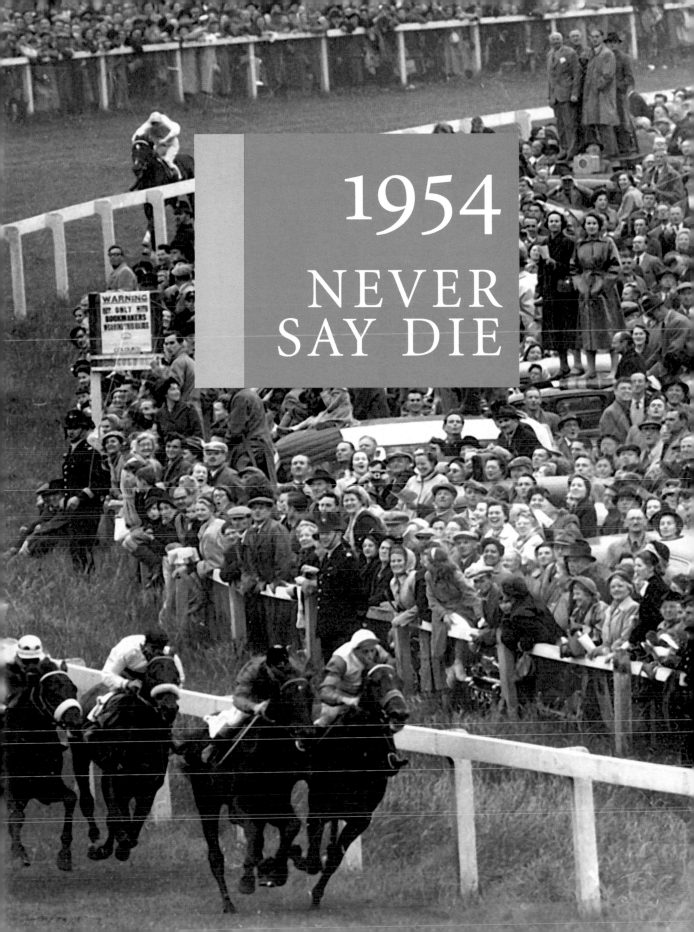

1954
NEVER
SAY DIE

Previous pages:
The 1954 Derby field at Tattenham Corner. Rowston Manor (Doug Smith, white cap) leads from the Queen's colt Landau (Willie Snaith), with Darius (Manny Mercer) on the rail and Blue Sail (Johnny Longden) on his outside. Lester is in fifth place on the white-faced Never Say Die.

175th Derby Stakes

2 June 1954
going: good
£16,959 10s to winner

1	**NEVER SAY DIE**	**L. Piggott**	**33–1**
2	ARABIAN NIGHT	T. Gosling	33–1
3	DARIUS	E. Mercer	7–1
4	ELOPEMENT	C. Smirke	9–1
5	Narrator	F. Barlow	66–1
6	Blue Prince II	W. H. Carr	33–1
7	Rowston Manor	D. Smith	5-1 jt fav
8	Landau	W. Snaith	100–7
9	L'Avengro	E. Smith	25–1
10	Blue Sail	J. Longden	100–6
11	Ferriol	W. R. Johnstone	5-1 jt fav
12	Moonlight Express	J. Mercer	50–1
13	Blue Rod	F. Durr	33–1
14	Kingsloe	W. Anderson	100–1
15	Court Splendour	W. Nevett	28–1
16	Alpenhorn	M. Beary	40–1
17	Hylas	F. Payne	100–1
18	Dark Corsair	J. Marshall	100–1
19	Valerullah	K. Gethin	100–9
20	Ruwenzori	E. Britt	66–1
21	Rokimos	J. Egan	100–1
p.u.	Cloonroughan	W. Rickaby	50–1

22 ran
distances: 2 lengths, neck
time: 2 minutes 35.8 seconds
Winner owned and bred by Robert Sterling Clark,
trained at Newmarket by Joe Lawson

'I'm going to ride that horse.' When towards the end of May 1954 Lester Piggott phoned the *Daily Express* racing journalist and BBC television commentator Peter O'Sullevan and made that announcement, O'Sullevan knew exactly which horse he meant: Never Say Die, then a 100–1 outsider for the Derby, less than a fortnight away. O'Sullevan duly filed his *Express* copy on the story, and in his autobiography *Calling the Horses* drily notes: 'I did not appreciate how limited would be future opportunity to obtain three-figure odds about L. Piggott riding the winner of the world's premier Classic.'

* * *

Bred by his owner, the hugely wealthy American tycoon Robert Sterling Clark, Never Say Die was conceived in Ireland, where his sire Nasrullah was standing as a stallion in 1950, but born in the USA. Third in the 1943 Derby, Nasrullah had been a brilliant but temperamental racehorse whose quirks were often passed on to his offspring: Zucchero, for example, who had given Lester such an uncomfortable start to his Derby career in 1951, was a son of Nasrullah. Never Say Die's dam Singing Grass was a daughter of the great American horse War Admiral, whose match with Seabiscuit in 1938 is the stuff of racing – and more recently cinematic – legend, but despite her elevated breeding she had managed to win in England only at a very humble level.

Like so many high-achieving horses, Never Say Die was blessed in his connections, though in terms of their years both owner and trainer provided a stark contrast to the youthful Lester Piggott, eighteen years old when Never Say Die ran at Epsom.

Robert Sterling Clark had been a great supporter of racing in Britain since 1930, and following a dispute with the American racing authorities after the war had decided to base his racing interests (though not all his breeding concerns) in Europe. By 1954 he was seventy-eight years old, and had already tasted Classic success, winning the One Thousand Guineas and Oaks in 1939 with the filly Galatea II, a half sister to Never Say Die's maternal granddam Boreale.

Trainer Joe Lawson was seventy-three, and coming towards the end of a distinguished career which by then had brought him ten Classic winners, beginning with Pennycomequick in the 1929 Oaks and including Galatea II's 1939 double. Among his other big-race successes were consecutive Ascot Gold Cups in 1931 and 1932 with Trimdon. Born in 1881, Lawson had tried to make his mark as a jockey before becoming too heavy, and in 1898 joined the famous trainer Alec Taylor at Manton as travelling head lad and later assistant trainer. When Taylor retired in 1927 Lawson took over at Manton, and was leading trainer in 1931 and 1936. After the war he moved from Manton to Carlburg Stables in Newmarket (currently Clive Brittain's yard). By the early 1950s the training of Robert Sterling Clark's horses was shared between Lawson and Harry Peacock, and in 1952 Peacock won the toss of a coin for first choice of the new crop of yearlings. He liked the look of the son of Singing Grass but disliked Nasrullah as a sire, so Never Say Die went to Joe Lawson.

Despite his wayward sire, Never Say Die, a compactly built chestnut with a large white blaze, proved a perfectly straightforward and amenable horse – if not, as a two-year-old, an outstandingly good one. Of his six races as a juvenile (in none of which was he ridden by Lester), he won just one, the Rosslyn Stakes at Ascot in July 1953. But he ran well enough in some of the leading two-year-old events – third in both the Richmond Stakes at Goodwood and the Dewhurst Stakes at Newmarket – to offer his connections some (though not much) hope for the 1954 Classics.

In *Racehorses of 1953* Phil Bull assessed the colt's three-year-old prospects with these words: 'Never Say Die, who is a very good looker, is clearly at least a stone below the top of the tree, and unless he shows abnormal improvement he would not therefore merit consideration for any of the Classic races. However, he is certain to make a goodish horse as a three-year-old.'

Never Say Die's first outing in 1954 came in the Union Jack Stakes at Liverpool in late March. In those days the Flat season began at the now defunct racecourse at Lincoln, where the feature of the opening meeting was the Lincolnshire Handicap. As soon as the Lincoln fixture was over, the racing community decamped to Liverpool for the three-day meeting which featured the Grand National, the world's most famous steeplechase, but which in those days consisted mostly of Flat races.

In 1951 Peter (now Sir Peter) O'Sullevan had been about to leave his home in London for the drive to Lincoln when he received a phone call

from Keith Piggott: 'Can you look after the boy and give him a lift to Liverpool?' Sir Peter describes the journeys in his Riley Pathfinder which began a lifelong friendship: 'We'd set off from Lincoln as soon as the last race had been run – or sooner if Lester didn't have a ride in the last – and stop at Macclesfield for me to phone over my copy to the *Express* while Lester sat quietly over a cup of tea. Then we headed over the Cat and Fiddle Pass – no motorways in those days, of course, and as often as not there was plenty of snow around – and stopped at the George at Knutsford for dinner before driving on to Liverpool, where like most of the racing crowd we always stayed at the Adelphi. Even in those days Lester was not one to engage in small talk. For most of the way over he'd be reading the paper, not only the racing pages, which he consumed avidly, but the financial pages and all the rest of the paper as well. I've never seen anyone read a newspaper as closely as Lester!'

By the start of the Flat in March 1954 Lester had already notched up some notable successes that spring. Having started riding over hurdles the previous autumn, he rode Mull Sack to win the Birdlip Hurdle, opening race of the National Hunt Meeting at Cheltenham (now the Cheltenham Festival), then four days later rode Prince Charlemagne, on whom he had been unplaced in the 1953 Derby, to an easy success in the Triumph Hurdle at Hurst Park. Prince Charlemagne's victory was the most important of the twenty hurdle winners ridden by Lester between December 1953 and February 1959, and those twenty winners came from just fifty-four National Hunt rides, an extraordinary strike rate of 37 per cent.

But the Flat was by a long way his first priority. In 1954 he did not ride a winner at the three-day Lincoln meeting, but on the trip across the Pennines he was hopeful of faring better at Liverpool. 'As usual he didn't talk much on the drive,' recalls Sir Peter O'Sullevan, 'but he was certainly looking forward to riding Never Say Die. He told me that the Lawson stable thought a great deal of the colt, though nobody else seriously entertained the possibility that he could win the Derby.'

* * *

The Liverpool race was the first time I sat on Never Say Die, though I was getting quite a few rides for Joe Lawson. I liked the colt immediately: he was very straightforward, simplicity itself to ride. For that first outing he was far from wound up to full fitness, and in the circumstances did very well to finish second, beaten only a length by Tudor Honey, ridden by my cousin Bill Rickaby. Never Say Die then ran in the Free Handicap at Newmarket, where he started favourite but never got into the race and finished in the ruck. This was disappointing, and we were beginning to feel that the idea of running the colt in the Derby should be dropped. But at the same time we were becoming convinced that Never Say Die's strong suit was stamina, and the seven furlongs of the Free Handicap could well have been too sharp for him. His next outing was back at the Rowley Mile over a mile and a quarter in the Newmarket Stakes, the

same race that Pinza had won a year earlier before going on to win the Derby. I was booked for some promising rides at Bath that day, so the ride on Never Say Die went to the late Manny Mercer. Never Say Die took the lead coming out of the Dip, but was run out of it close home and finished third behind Elopement and Golden God, beaten half a length and a head. (My trip to Bath, by the way, was well worth it, as I rode three winners over the two days of the meeting.)

The Newmarket performance was fairly encouraging, but after the race Manny Mercer reported that the horse had hung badly, and Mr Clark's British representative Gerald McElligott sent a cable to him in the USA suggesting that Never Say Die be scratched from the Derby, as with his habit of hanging to the right – which is what McElligott understood Manny to have said – he would have no chance round the left-handed bends of Epsom. Mr Clark wrote back to the effect that if this was the case then Never Say Die should indeed be taken out of the Derby – then shortly after posting that letter received another cable, this time from Joe Lawson, who had heard of Gerald McElligott's message and was desperate to correct it: Never Say Die had hung to the left, not the right, and therefore had been kept in the Derby. Mr Clark agreed that the horse should run, but it was a measure of his lack of confidence that he decided not to travel over for the race, having booked himself into a health farm for the week when the Derby was being run.

Whatever the rights or lefts of the situation, the bookmakers were less than impressed, and Never Say Die was still readily available at 200–1 in the ante-post market for the big race.

In all honesty, it was difficult to argue with such an assessment: strictly on form he had a good deal to find to be a true Derby prospect. Then his home work at Newmarket started to improve significantly, and a week before the Derby he produced an exceptional gallop. All of a sudden the stable's hope was transformed to optimism, but that optimism proved less than infectious when it came to finding a jockey for the Derby. My going to Bath rather than riding the horse at Newmarket had not made me first choice as far as Joe Lawson was concerned, and he asked Manny Mercer to ride Never Say Die at Epsom. Manny was already committed and had to decline. So Charlie Smirke was approached, but he couldn't be tempted to take the ride. I think one other jockey was asked and gave the same response, and that left me. I accepted.

Never Say Die's inclination to hang to the left had led the stable to try out all sorts of corrective devices on him, such as special bits, but I persuaded them to leave these off for the race, as I knew that hanging left-handed could prove an advantage.

Some newspaper accounts of the 1954 Derby told the story of how, when being driven to Epsom by my father on the morning of the race, I had confided in him that I had very little chance. Not for the last time, the press got it completely wrong. I was of course well aware that strictly on the form book Never Say Die seemed an unlikely Derby winner, but I was expecting a major improvement on his previous efforts. What I did discuss with my father was the best way to approach the race from a tactical point of view, and we agreed that the horse to track would be Darius, winner of the Two Thousand Guineas. He was clearly a horse of some class, although there were questions over his stamina.

That doubt about Darius lasting home made him only third favourite in the betting for what appeared a very open race. Joint favourites of the twenty-two runners – the smallest Derby field I'd yet ridden in – were Rowston Manor, who had won the Derby Trial at Lingfield Park, and the French-trained Ferriol, runner-up to Darius in the Two Thousand Guineas. Both started at 5–1, while Darius himself went off at 7–1 and Sir Victor Sassoon's Elopement, who had beaten Never Say Die at Newmarket, at 9–1. The Queen's colt Landau, a son of the triple Classic-winning mare Sun Chariot who had been well beaten in the Guineas then finished runner-up to Rowston Manor in the Lingfield Derby Trial, started at 100–7 to go one better than Her Majesty's Aureole, runner-up to Pinza in 1953. Never Say Die himself started an outsider at 33–1 (a good deal shorter than his odds a fortnight earlier), the same price as Arabian Night, who had run fourth in the Two Thousand Guineas and finished behind Never Say Die in the Newmarket Stakes.

* * *

Most of the newspaper pundits gave Never Say Die little chance, though more than one recommended the colt for once-a-year punters who liked to back an outsider with an appealing name. He did have some lukewarm support from the experts, however. On the morning of the race the *Daily Telegraph* declared: 'Never Say Die may have been a trifle unlucky when third to Elopement at Newmarket. He has given every satisfaction in his work since and should run a good race.'

As always, much of the press prognostication in advance of the race centred on how well the fancied horses would act on the Epsom track, for one of the major factors which makes the Derby a unique test of a young racehorse is the course itself, which is unlike any other terrain in world racing. (See page 239.)

The race starts opposite the stands, with an uphill stretch climbing towards the first bend, a gradual right-hander, after which the runners tack across to the inside rail to continue the climb towards the top of the hill, which they reach at about the halfway point of their mile-and-a-half trip. From the summit the course sweeps down in a left-handed arc, the helter-skelter gradient becoming steeper as the runners approach Tattenham Corner. That famous turn takes them into the straight just under half a mile from the winning post, and they continue on a gradual downhill gradient until the ground rises slightly with about a hundred yards to go. The final trick up the sleeve of the Derby course is the slope of the ground from the stands side to inside all the way up the straight, a significant camber which can cause tired horses to hang to their left.

*   *   *

I'd ridden three runners in the Derby before Never Say Die, and it didn't take long for me to appreciate that from a jockey's point of

Age before youth. Fifty-six-year-old Alf Vaus leads Lester and Never Say Die out of the paddock before the Derby.

view it is an especially difficult race. The peculiar nature of the course is obviously a major factor in that, but far from the only one. The status of the race is such that owners and trainers are desperately keen to have a runner, with the result that it attracts more no-hopers than other big races, and the trouble with no-hopers is that when they start to fall back beaten they get in the way of the better horses looking to improve their position. At Epsom this problem is compounded by the course, as those outsiders start to give up the ghost soon after the top of the hill, and are back-pedalling on the long downhill stretch. This explains why the Derby is so often a very rough race, and why the crucial tactic for any horse with a decent chance is to be close up all the way, and no worse than seventh or eighth on the descent to Tattenham Corner. There have been cases of horses coming from way back to win the Derby, but not many.

The finish head on: Never Say Die, Arabian Night (Tommy Gosling, quartered cap) and Darius (Manny Mercer) well clear of the rest.

Previous pages:
*The finish side on:
Never Say Die two
lengths ahead of
Arabian Night, with
Darius almost obscured
in third.*

Of course, you can plan your tactics as long as you like, but you still have to have the sort of horse who can carry them out, and for me size always mattered much less in a Derby horse than his manner of racing. What you need most of all is a type who can lay up handy behind the leaders during the first half mile and stay in that position at least until Tattenham Corner. If you fall too far behind it is usually disastrous, as there's no part of the course where you can readily make up lost ground.

In many ways Never Say Die was the ideal Derby horse – physically compact and very well balanced, and temperamentally equipped to put up with all the distractions of the long drawn out preliminaries. In addition, there was his left-handed bias.

On an overcast and cold Derby day (the Queen wore a mink stole), I was able to ride the race exactly as I wanted. Doug Smith on Rowston Manor had difficulty settling his colt, and after a furlong he had pulled his way to the front, where he set the pace with L'Avengro (ridden by Doug's brother Eph) and Blue Sail (ridden by the great American jockey Johnny Longden). Never Say Die sat in behind the leaders throughout the early stages, came down the hill smoothly, and at Tattenham Corner was perfectly placed in fifth on the outside behind Rowston Manor, Landau, Darius and Blue Sail. Once into the straight Blue Sail weakened and fell back, but neither Rowston Manor nor Landau could hold their positions for long, and I eased Never Say Die forward as Darius took the lead with a quarter of a mile to go. Never Say Die was going so well that he swept past Darius in a matter of strides, and, after I had allowed myself the luxury of a quick look round to check that nothing was catching me from behind, that was that. Arabian Night finished strongly to beat Darius a neck for second place, with Elopement fourth, but Never Say Die's winning margin of two lengths was hardly an adequate measure of his superiority.

People talk about the Derby as the ultimate challenge for horse and jockey, but this race could hardly have been simpler – which perhaps accounts for my lack of visible ecstasy as we passed the post. (One newspaper even had a front-page photograph of me just past the winning post with my eyes closed.) The fact is that never at any point in my career did I allow myself to appear overjoyed after winning any race, big or small, and however much the press demanded it, I could not and would not manufacture elation. Never Say Die's Derby victory gave me the satisfaction of a job well and properly done, but that was all. (I have to admit, though, that I was quite keen to see for myself just how well the job had been done, and a week after the Derby made an arrangement with the manager of a cinema in Reading for a private showing of a recording of the race.)

Tradition dictates that the Derby winner is led into the winner's enclosure by his owner, but as Mr Clark was not present Never Say

A beaming Lester is led in after the race.

Die was led in by the stable lad who looked after him, Alfie Vaus. Mr Clark later described himself as 'completely flabbergasted' by the result, and while many were of a similar opinion, I was not quite as surprised. The colt had the ideal physical and mental make-up, and never really had his ideal conditions in a race until he ran in the Derby.

I had one more ride that afternoon, winning the final race of the day on Damremont. Then I was driven home to Lambourn by my parents, spent an hour mowing the lawn, and as usual was in bed soon after 9 p.m.

* * *

The rest of the racing world did not treat the sensation of an eighteen-year-old winning the Derby quite so casually.

Lester was the youngest jockey to ride the Derby winner in the twentieth century, and possibly the youngest ever: records of the early runnings are sketchy and the exact age of winning riders cannot always be verified with any confidence. John Randall, resident historian at the *Racing Post* and the racing anorak's anorak, notes that John Parsons was alleged to have been sixteen years old when winning the 1862 running on Caractacus, and suggests that Lester was probably the second-youngest winning rider in the history of the race.

In any event, the niceties of the historical record did not bother the racing press in 1954. As far as they were concerned Lester was the youngest ever, and had turned in an astonishingly confident and assured ride in the most difficult race in the calendar. John Rickman, 'Robin Goodfellow' in the *Daily Mail,* enthused: 'What a triumph for this brilliant boy. His tenacity and will to win sometimes gets him into trouble, but it has earned him the Turf's highest prize at the comparatively tender age of eighteen.' In the *Daily Express,* Clive Graham described how in the straight 'Lester had the race at his mercy and he went about his job with an unhurried authority which stamped the hallmark on his brilliant meteor-like rise to riding fame.'

But journalists fishing for 'over the moon'-type comments from the hero of the hour were – not for the last time in Lester's career – disappointed.

The *Daily Telegraph* contacted him at home on the evening of the Derby and was told: 'We are not having a special party or celebration. It is just an ordinary evening for me. I shall be in bed at 9.15 p.m. and will be up at 7 a.m. tomorrow … I had a lovely ride all the way today and I won easily. I would not say it is the greatest day of my life, but Never Say Die's win gave me a great thrill.'

The result also gave a great thrill to the bookmakers crowded into the enclosures and up on the Downs. Layer Douglas Stuart declared: 'In my fifty years in business, I cannot recall a worse Derby result for backers, and that is another way of saying it's my best Derby. A few bets were placed on the winner by those attracted by the name, but the big backers hardly gave him a second thought.' Alfred Cope, in those days one of the biggest bookmakers in the betting ring, called the result a perfect one for the small punter: 'After all, how could he miss with a horse called Never Say Die?'

Never Say Die provided Lester not only with his first Derby winner but with his first winner of any of the five English Classics — Two Thousand Guineas, One Thousand Guineas, Derby, Oaks and St Leger — which form the landmark events of the Flat season for three-year-olds. His final Classic winner was to come nearly thirty-eight years later on Rodrigo de Triano in the 1992 Two Thousand Guineas, and his tally of thirty Classic victories is another racing record achieved by Lester which is unlikely to be beaten.

Four of the other runners in the 1954 Derby went on to distinguish themselves in later races. Darius confirmed himself a top-class horse over shorter distances, and won the 1955 Eclipse Stakes (ridden by Lester). Landau won the Rous Memorial Stakes at Royal Ascot and the Sussex Stakes at Goodwood later in 1954. Narrator, well beaten in the Derby, won the Champion Stakes at Newmarket late in the 1954 season at 20–1, and returned to Epsom in 1955 to land the Coronation Cup. Elopement, fourth in the Derby and narrowly beaten by Narrator in the Champion Stakes, won the Hardwicke Stakes at Royal Ascot in 1955, ridden by Lester for trainer Noel Murless.

Never Say Die himself was only the second American-bred Derby winner, after Iroquois (ridden by Fred Archer) in 1881. He was clearly the best three-year-old of his generation, but in his first race after the Derby,

the King Edward VII Stakes at Royal Ascot some two weeks later on 17 June, he did not even start favourite. Arabian Night, second at Epsom at level weights, was now carrying eight pounds less than the Derby winner, enough to make him a narrow market leader at 13–8, with Lester and Never Say Die at 7–4; Rashleigh, trained by Noel Murless and ridden by Sir Gordon Richards, was third favourite at 5–1. This famously rough race, run on the third day of the four-day Royal meeting, proved a turning point in Lester's career.

* * *

So much has been written about this race that it's unnecessary to go over it all again in detail. Suffice it to say that early in the short Ascot home straight I found myself stuck in fourth place behind Rashleigh on the outside, Dragon Fly (ridden by Doug Smith) and Garter (Bill Rickaby). Never Say Die was full of running, so when a gap opened between Dragon Fly on the inner and Garter, I tried to push Never Say Die through it. Just at that moment Gordon tried to manoeuvre Rashleigh towards the inner, which caused Garter to be squeezed up and bumped on both sides. After a few seconds of argy-bargy we sorted ourselves out, but Never Say Die had suffered in the scrimmaging and could finish only fourth behind Rashleigh, with Tarjoman and Blue Prince II (neither of whom had been involved in the incident) second and third.

I was summoned to appear before the Ascot stewards, who solemnly informed me that they held me responsible for the fracas as I had been going for a gap when there was no gap to go for, and told me I was suspended for the rest of the meeting and had to face the Stewards of the Jockey Club the following morning. This was particularly bad news, as it's fair to say that my disciplinary record during the first few years of my riding career had not been exemplary and I'd had several previous suspensions. I knew I was in for something more than a rap on the knuckles, but even so it was a shock when the Jockey Club Stewards told me that they were withdrawing my licence for the rest of the season. They told my father — with whom I was still based at the time, though I was no longer formally an apprentice — that henceforth I would have to be connected to a stable other than his.

I was furious about what was tantamount to being warned off, but there was little I could do about it so I had to go along with the sentence and concentrate on rebuilding my career when I got my licence back — which in the event I did before the end of the 1954 season, as the sentence was commuted. But by then it was too late for me to ride Never Say Die again, and it was particularly galling to be sidelined when Charlie Smirke won the St Leger on him: Never Say Die scooted home by twelve lengths in the manner of a really great horse, and luckily this time Mr Clark was there to see his horse win.

At one point it looked as if Never Say Die would run in the Jockey Club Stakes at Newmarket at the end of September, by which time I had got my licence back and would have been able to ride him. But Mr Clark and the Queen were running very close for the title of leading owner that season, and victory for Never Say Die in the Newmarket race would have secured the title. So Mr Clark generously withdrew the colt, leaving the Queen to become leading owner for the first time.

* * *

That was not Robert Sterling Clark's only magnanimous gesture. As a token of his regard for the British Turf he presented Never Say Die to the National Stud, then based at Gillingham in Dorset. (It did not move to its present location in Newmarket until 1967.) Never Say Die became one of the select band of Derby winners who have themselves sired a Derby winner when his son Larkspur won in 1962 in the colours of Raymond Guest and trained by Vincent O'Brien (six years later owner and trainer of Lester's fourth Derby winner Sir Ivor). His offspring also included the brilliant filly Never Too Late II, winner of the One Thousand Guineas and Oaks in 1960. Never Say Die was put down in 1975 at the age of twenty-four.

Robert Sterling Clark died in 1956, and Joe Lawson, for whom Never Say Die's St Leger victory meant that he had trained winners of all five Classics, in 1964.

A curious postscript to the Never Say Die story was written in 1996, forty-two years after his great triumph at Epsom, when Sotheby's auction house in London included in its sale of racing works of art and memorabilia Lot 331: 'Racing silks worn by Lester Piggott, believed to have been worn on the occasion of his first Derby win in 1954 on Never Say Die'. The estimated price was given as £300 to £500, but they fetched £5,520 from a private collector bidding over the telephone. Not long after the sale, doubt was cast on whether these were the actual silks worn by Lester on 2 June 1954, but the purchaser decided to keep them whether they were genuine or not – further evidence of the historic resonance of the Derby victory of Never Say Die.

Never Say Die

Pedigree

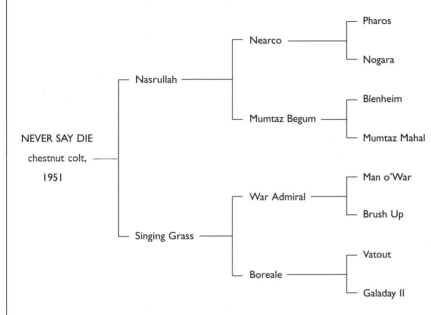

NEVER SAY DIE
chestnut colt,
1951

- Nasrullah
  - Nearco
    - Pharos
    - Nogara
  - Mumtaz Begum
    - Blenheim
    - Mumtaz Mahal
- Singing Grass
  - War Admiral
    - Man o'War
    - Brush Up
  - Boreale
    - Vatout
    - Galaday II

Racing Record

Year	Race	Course	Jockey	Position
1953	May Maiden Stakes	Newmarket	P. Newson	6th
	New Stakes	Ascot	A. Breasley	6th
	Rosslyn Stakes	**Ascot**	**E. Mercer**	**won**
	Richmond Stakes	Goodwood	A. Breasley	3rd
	Solario Stakes	Sandown Park	A. Breasley	5th
	Dewhurst Stakes	Newmarket	A. Breasley	3rd
1954	Union Jack Stakes	Liverpool	L. Piggott	2nd
	Free Handicap	Newmarket	L. Piggott	unplaced
	Newmarket Stakes	Newmarket	E. Mercer	3rd
	DERBY STAKES	**Epsom**	**L. Piggott**	**won**
	King Edward VII Stakes	Ascot	L. Piggott	4th
	St Leger Stakes	**Doncaster**	**C. Smirke**	**won**

ran in 12 races, won 3

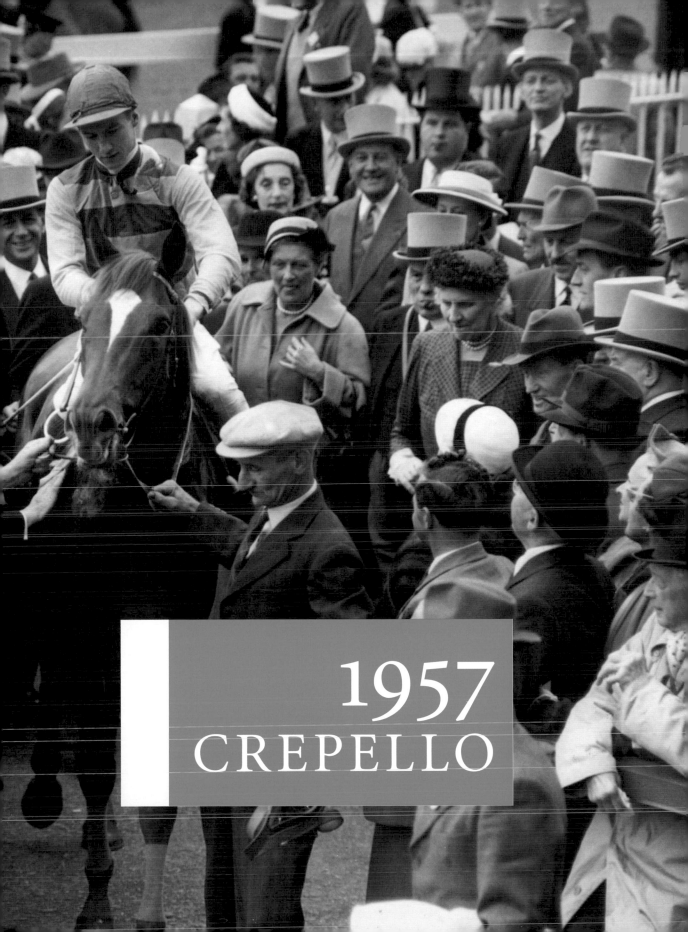

1957
CREPELLO

Previous pages:
Sir Victor Sassoon leads Crepello and Lester into the winner's circle.

178th Derby Stakes

5 June 1957
going: firm
£18,659 10s to winner

1	**CREPELLO**	**L. Piggott**	**6–4 fav**
2	BALLYMOSS	T. P. Burns	33–1
3	PIPE OF PEACE	A. Breasley	100–8
4	TEMPEST	W. Rickaby	28–1
5	Royaumont	J. Deforge	100–9
6	Messmate	E. Mercer	25–1
7	Apostol	J. Doyasbere	18–1
8	Albergo	J. Mercer	45–1
9	Prince Taj	J. Massard	10–1
10	Doutelle	W. H. Carr	100–6
11	Brioche	E. Hide	50–1
12	Chevastrid	J. Eddery	50–1
13	Palor	F. Durr	33–1
14	Lightehran	W. Snaith	50–1
15	London Cry	D. Smith	18–1
16	Mystic Prince	B. Swift	100–1
17	Alcastus	C. Smirke	33–1
18	Hedonist	K. Gethin	100–1
19	Barred Rock	D. Ryan	100–1
20	Eudaemon	E. Britt	45–1
21	Chippendale	W. R. Johnstone	100–7
22	Bois de Miel	E. J. Cracknell	100–1

22 ran
distances 1½ lengths, 1 length
time: 2 minutes 35.4 seconds
Winner owned and bred by Sir Victor Sassoon,
trained at Newmarket by Noel Murless

Like Never Say Die, Lester's next two rides in the Derby started at 33–1. Unlike Never Say Die, both ran a race which justified such odds. In 1955 he rode Windsor Sun, trained in Ireland by Seamus McGrath. The colt had been well beaten in the Two Thousand Guineas, and at Epsom finished down the field behind the French-trained winner Phil Drake, ridden by Freddie Palmer.

The following year Lester fared little better on Affiliation Order, officially trained at Blewbury by Charles Jerdein but in fact in the charge of Helen Johnson Houghton, twin sister of the great National Hunt trainer Fulke Walwyn. Back in those Dark Ages ladies were not allowed to hold training licences, so it was Jerdein's name which appeared in the records – and which earlier in the 1956 season had been credited with training Two Thousand Guineas winner Gilles de Retz. Affiliation Order had not run as a two-year-old, but in May made a promising racecourse debut when winning a small race at Newmarket, ridden by Lester. Later that month the Australian jockey Scobie Breasley rode the colt to win another modest event, this time at Hurst Park. The notion of an unbeaten colt tackling the Derby clearly appealed to the proprietors of the *Daily Sketch*, who in an early version of the present-day habit of newspapers taking over horses for big races offered ownership of Affiliation Order on Derby Day as the prize in a competition. Booking Lester for the ride clearly added to the allure of the prize, but in the race itself the competition winner did not have his hopes raised too far. Affiliation Order was never in the hunt, and finished well back behind another French-trained winner, Lavandin.

A couple of weeks after the 1956 Derby, Lester rode a colt at Royal Ascot who within a year would be counted one of his very best Derby winners: Crepello.

In July 1954, while Lester had been serving out his suspension following the Never Say Die incident at Ascot, Gordon Richards suffered very bad injuries when a horse named Abergeldie reared and fell backwards on him in the Sandown Park parade ring. Soon afterwards came the inevitable news of the great jockey's retirement, which created a vacancy as stable jockey to Noel Murless, the leading trainer in Britain and Richards's main retainer. Though only eighteen years old and still under the cloud of the suspension, Lester was the obvious candidate for the best riding job in British racing. But before Lester – then, as later, never shy of making a phone call to see whether his services might be required — could contact Murless, a complication arose: Gordon Richards himself was setting up as a trainer and asked Lester to be his stable jockey. Lester decided to delay replying to Richards until he had approached Murless, and on hearing that Murless did indeed want to take him on, there was only one career path: up Newmarket's Warren Hill to Warren Place. Ironically, one of Lester's first winners as Murless's stable jockey in the autumn of 1954 was Rashleigh, who had been a leading player in that notorious King Edward VII Stakes.

Noel Murless, born in 1910, had learned his trade with the Irish trainer Hubert Hartigan before starting his own operation in 1935 in Hambleton in Yorkshire, moving in 1947 to the famous yard of Beckhampton, near Marlborough in Wiltshire. It was here that he was based when winning his first trainers' championship in 1948, the year of his first Classic victory, with Queenpot in the One Thousand Guineas. The following year he won the St Leger with Ridge Wood, but his most famous charge in the late 1940s was the great sprinter Abernant. By the time Lester joined him at Warren Place he had been at Newmarket only two years. (Warren Place is now in the charge of Henry Cecil, a trainer with whom Lester would later be closely associated; Cecil's first wife was Noel Murless's daughter Julie.)

A chestnut colt by the Italian sire Donatello II, Crepello was home-bred by his owner Sir Victor Sassoon, whose quest for a Derby winner had gone on for many years and cost him many hundreds of thousands of pounds. His colt Hot Night had been runner-up to Call Boy in 1927, and ten years after that his filly Exhibitionnist (trained by Joe Lawson) had won the One Thousand Guineas and Oaks, but it was not until 1953 that he finally reached his Holy Grail of owning the Derby winner with the victory of Pinza, ridden by Gordon Richards and trained by Norman Bertie. The following year Noel Murless, who had previously acted as a bloodstock adviser, started training for him.

Crepello's dam Crepuscule was a very ordinary racehorse herself (she won only one small race), but has the rare distinction of having bred two Classic winners from her first two foals: her first was the filly Honeylight, who won the 1956 One Thousand Guineas, and her second was Crepello. Her later offspring included Twilight Alley, on whom Lester won the Ascot Gold Cup in 1963.

* * *

Crepello was particularly well made and sturdy, but he was somewhat heavy-shouldered and his forelegs were rather straight: for that reason you would not have immediately picked him out as an ideal Derby horse, as types like that often get jarred up at Epsom. As protection for his delicate forelegs, Crepello was fitted with cloths made of some soft fabric which were sewn round to protect the cannon bone and tendons: these were regularly rotated round each leg to remove dust and dirt which might have found its way in.

Because of his good looks and general presence Crepello was immediately a great favourite in the yard and the apple of Noel Murless's eye. Noel was convinced from the moment they started breaking in the colt that he would be a top-class performer, and once we started working him at speed it was obvious that he had real Classic potential. His breeding was full of stamina – Donatello II had sired two winners of the Ascot Gold Cup, Alycidon and Supertello – but Crepello showed enough speed at home to suggest he'd be well suited by the mile of the Two Thousand Guineas.

His first outing came in the Windsor Castle Stakes over five furlongs at Royal Ascot, where he started 11–2 third favourite and ran very well. Noel Murless always wanted his juveniles to be given a gentle introduction and – Royal Ascot or no Royal Ascot – my instructions were to be as easy on him as possible. After letting him settle in the early stages, we came with a real rattle in the final furlong and failed only by a head to catch Fulfer, a very speedy two-year-old trained by Geoffrey Brooke who had shown decent form in three previous outings. In the circumstances it was a highly encouraging debut by Crepello.

That race was in June, and Crepello did not race again until the middle of October, in the six-furlong Middle Park Stakes at Newmarket, when he ran well to finish fourth behind Pipe Of Peace, trained by Gordon Richards and ridden by Scobie Breasley (who had taken the job as Gordon's stable jockey after I had declined it). Stamina was always likely to be Crepello's strong suit, and when stepped up to seven furlongs two weeks later for the Dewhurst Stakes at Newmarket – the most prestigious two-year-old race of the season – he started odds-on favourite against just three opponents, and was hardly out of a canter to win cosily from the Queen's colt Doutelle.

*   *   *

One win from three races as a juvenile, but Crepello was clearly a colt of the highest potential – as testified by the opinion of Phil Bull in his assessment of Crepello's future in *Racehorses of 1956*:

> More than most of his age Crepello gives the impression that he has abundant scope for future development, and even in October he was not really well muscled up or well furnished. If evidence is forthcoming in his three-year-old season that this promise of improvement has been maintained, he will be a very live prospect indeed. These are, however, very early days to assess any horse's chances in the Derby or St Leger, but Crepello's performances suggest that he is a colt very much out of the ordinary, and one with Classic potentialities as high as those of any two-year-old that raced in 1956. He looks like making an exceptionally good long-distance horse, and appears to be the ideal animal for the 1957 St Leger, and the following year's Gold Cup. Although he came down the hill at Newmarket quite well in his last race, it is very much to be doubted whether he is the sort of horse who will be at home on the long, downhill stretch round Tattenham Corner, particularly if the going on Derby day should be firm.

At this period Peter O'Sullevan's 'Stable Tour' reports in the *Daily Express* were a keenly anticipated part of the build-up toward the start of the Flat season each March: his travels around the leading training stables at home and abroad unearthed many a horse to follow for the months ahead. In March 1957 he reported his findings at Newmarket:

> If you draw a straight line, add a small circle with a tail at an acute angle to the left, then write 'CHC' above or below, you have the Newmarket work-watchers' shorthand version of 'Crepello'.
>
>   The circle indicates white on Crepello's forehead; the tail represents

white running down his nose; the 'CHC' that he is a chestnut colt; and the horizontal line that he has a body.

Some body – and one which may well end up in the winner's circle after the Two Thousand Guineas and/or Derby if the French invasion is to be repulsed. And needless to say, this will be Lester Piggott's Classics ride.

O'Sullevan was right on all counts.

*   *   *

It was Noel Murless's custom not to canter his horses through the close season, but give them an easy time in the coldest months of the year before they began trotting in January and cantering in February. Crepello thrived over the winter, and by the time we started his serious build-up towards the Classics had grown to over 16.2 hands.

Crepello went into the 1957 Two Thousand Guineas without a preliminary race, and one home gallop in particular had convinced Noel that the horse would be fit enough without a previous run: we worked him over a mile with some decent older horses, one of which was Kandy Sauce, who the previous year had easily won the Queen Anne Stakes at Royal Ascot, and Crepello galloped all over them. Indeed, he was so impressive that Noel, who very rarely had a bet, staked £100 at 66–1 that Crepello would win the Two Thousand Guineas and Derby.

At one point it had been the plan to run him in the Guineas trial at Kempton Park, and then in a similar race at Epsom, but in the event it was decided that he was not forward enough for either. His work at home had been outstanding, though one slightly worrying trait which was beginning to appear was a tendency to pull very hard.

The plan for the Two Thousand Guineas was to keep Crepello well off the pace and make ground once we had got to the Bushes – in those days a notable landmark on the Rowley Mile, on the far side of the course about two furlongs from the finish, and just before the descent into the Dip. On the day everything went beautifully. The going was officially hard and the distance supposedly short of what

Crepello needed, and he started 7–2 second favourite, with Pipe Of Peace, who had beaten us in the Middle Park the previous year and earlier in the spring of 1957 had won the Greenham Stakes at Newbury, a little shorter at 100–30. We were drawn 15 of the fifteen runners – on the far side of the track – which was supposedly a disadvantage, but I was able to work Crepello over towards the stands side and roust him up as we raced into the Dip. He hit the front with about a furlong to go but I had to keep him up to his work as first Pipe Of Peace and then Quorum – later to secure lasting fame as sire of Red Rum – launched their challenges. It was close, but we were never going to be headed on the run to the line, and at the winning post Crepello was half a length in front of Quorum, with Pipe Of Peace just a head away in third. Given Crepello's breeding and conformation, this was a great victory, and a bonus: the Derby and St Leger lay ahead.

* * *

In the weeks after the Two Thousand Guineas, Crepello's Derby preparation proceeded without hitch. The price of 3–1 available about him just after the Guineas soon shortened to 7–4, despite the occasional outbreak of the sort of rumour which a big-race favourite traditionally attracts, and the news that the leading French challenger Mourne, who had won the Prix Lupin, had broken down in the Prix Daru and would not race again made Crepello an even hotter favourite.

On Friday 31 May, five days before the Derby the following Wednesday, fresh gossip started spreading around the race crowd at Sandown Park that all was not well with the colt, and at the 'callover' that evening his price eased to 2–1. The following morning's *Daily Express* carried Peter O'Sullevan's sardonic reflections on a day of rumour:

> Continuing the Crepello serial … 'they' went to work with the whispers once again at Sandown yesterday, when 'they' said that 10–1 – and more in places – was available about the favourite.
>
> 'They' didn't say where the odds were offered, but 'they' all had it on pretty good authority that Crepello would not be in the Derby field on

Wednesday. A leading bookmaker declared that before midday he had been offered 'four monkeys' by a fellow layer.

He had not accepted the offer.

And in case you should be unfamiliar with the terminology and assume that bookmakers are now trading zoological specimens among themselves – 'four monkeys' in racing parlance means £2,000 to £500.

By one o'clock so many maladies had been ascribed to the unfortunate favourite that it seemed a positive unkindness not to put him out of his misery forthwith.

Roy Ullyett's take on the Crepello rumours in the Daily Express, *5 June 1957.*

* * *

I was vaguely aware of these rumours, but knew them to be complete nonsense: Crepello had worked wonderfully well since the Two Thousand Guineas, and we were going into the Derby full of confidence. As a precaution against any outside interference, guards were stationed at the door of his box at Warren Place in the days leading up to the race, but nothing untoward took place, and Crepello duly arrived at Epsom fit and well. The day before the race I took him for an early-morning gallop over the first part of the Derby course, but slowed down to allow him to walk down the hill and round Tattenham Corner and get a good look at his surroundings.

By Derby Day our confidence was apparently again shared by the public, and the betting market took on such a one-sided look – after all, who could beat Crepello? – that the starting prices had our colt favourite at 6–4 with the French-trained Prince Taj second favourite at 10–1.

Owned by the then Aga Khan – who had won the Derby five times, most recently with Tulyar in 1952 – Prince Taj owed his position in the market to some very good form in France, including a fast-finishing third in the Poule d'Essai des Poulains, the equivalent of the Two Thousand Guineas. Another French-trained contender was Royaumont, third favourite on 100–9, while Crepello's old rival Pipe Of Peace was considered unlikely to reverse Two Thousand Guineas form over the longer distance of the Derby and started at 100–8. The Queen's colt Doutelle, runner-up to Crepello in the Dewhurst Stakes, was unbeaten in his two outings as a three-year-old – the Two Thousand Guineas Trial at Kempton Park and the Lingfield Derby Trial – and started at 100–6.

Among the 33–1 shots was Ballymoss, a first Derby runner for Irish trainer Vincent O'Brien. At that time Vincent was best known as a National Hunt trainer, having won three consecutive Grand Nationals, and though I had met him I could not then claim to know him well. As a two-year-old Ballymoss had won just one of his four races, a maiden plate at Leopardstown, but had won in such a manner as to get Vincent thinking of aiming the colt at the 1957 Derby. Such a plan seemed somewhat ambitious when Ballymoss was unplaced in his first run of 1957, but he then won the Trigo Stakes at Leopardstown over a mile and a half at 20–1, with his stable companion Gladness the unplaced odds-on favourite. For all that, Ballymoss was pretty well unknown in England (and certainly unknown to me), though Peter O'Sullevan had had word from Ireland that the colt was no forlorn chance in the Derby and had been backing him each way at 100–1, 50–1 and 40–1.

The going on Derby Day was firm, which was not ideal for Crepello, given his conformation. He was very much on his toes during the preliminaries, but since this was by now fairly usual for him I was not in the least concerned. Crepello was drawn 2 – that is, one horse in from the inside – and I had to get him off the mark fairly briskly to avoid being cut off when the runners tacked back towards the inside rail after the first, right-handed, bend. He was a very easy horse to manage, and I had no problem getting his position and then settling him behind the leaders, a position we held throughout the first half of the race.

At Tattenham Corner we were sixth, one horse off the inside rail and about three lengths behind the leader Brioche. Ballymoss was just ahead of us but it seemed to me even at that stage that Crepello was travelling better than any other horse in the race. Two furlongs out Ballymoss took the lead, but Crepello had him well covered, and when with over a furlong to go I asked him to overtake the Irish horse he did so with the minimum of fuss, reeling in Ballymoss easily and cruising to the front. After the Guineas I was aware that he might idle a little once he had got

Tattenham Corner, 1957: Brioche (Edward Hide) leads, with Lester and Crepello in sixth place and Ballymoss (T. P. Burns) just ahead of them.

Previous pages:
*The 1957 finish:
Crepello wins easily
from Ballymoss, with
Pipe Of Peace (Scobie
Breasley, white cap)
third.*

*The winner's circle: Sir
Victor Sassoon is on the
left, with trainer Noel
Murless, back to the
camera, in the light grey
topper.*

to the front, so I pushed him out throughout most of the final furlong before easing up just before the winning post. He won by a length and a half from Ballymoss, and Pipe Of Peace ran on to finish third, having apparently suffered from scrimmaging on the run down the hill and getting himself into an impossible position at Tattenham Corner. Whatever trouble there had been, Crepello was not involved at all.

As Crepello was being led back to the winner's enclosure, someone broke through the crowd surrounding the horse and thrust a gold watch into my hand. It was the flamboyant society hairdresser Pierre 'Teasy Weasy' Raymond, who was a great friend of my father's and had horses in training with him (and who would later own two Grand National winners, one of them – Ayala in 1963 – trained by my father). In his excitement at Crepello's victory he had ripped the watch from his own wrist and insisted that I have it!

That was not the only present I received. Crepello was Sir Victor Sassoon's second Derby winner in five runnings, and he did not stint in his generosity to his winning jockey, making me a gift of his Lincoln Continental, the huge American car which he used only on his visits to

London – he lived for most of the year in the Bahamas – and which he thought I would make better use of than himself. I hadn't had the car very long when I ran into the back of another car one rainy night on the Great West Road in London. The other driver was unhurt, but the Lincoln needed a new radiator, which could not be bought in Britain and had to be sent from the USA. This made me think that the car might be more trouble than it was worth, so I sold it to the then Duke of Bedford, and he displayed it in his collection of cars at Woburn Abbey.

Two days later I won the Oaks by a short head on Carrozza, trained by Noel Murless and owned by the Queen – Her Majesty's first Classic winner. That was quite a week.

* * *

Crepello's victory in the Derby was a performance of the highest class – of a level which became more apparent as Ballymoss, whom he had beaten so easily, established himself as one of the greatest horses to race in Europe since the Second World War: later in 1957 Ballymoss won the Irish Derby and St Leger, and in 1958 the Coronation Cup, Eclipse Stakes, King George VI and Queen Elizabeth Stakes and Prix de l'Arc de Triomphe. A more immediate mark of the quality of the 1957 Derby is the time of the race: 2 minutes 35.4 seconds was the fastest time recorded since Mahmoud had set a new record of 2 minutes 33.8 seconds twenty-one years earlier in 1936. At 6–4, Crepello was the shortest priced Derby favourite since Tudor Minstrel had finished fourth at 4–7 in 1947, and the shortest priced winner of the race since Bahram at 5–4 in 1935.

The newspapers were suitably impressed. Tom Nickalls in the *Sporting Life* opened his report with the words: 'British bloodstock received the finest possible fillip when Sir Victor Sassoon's magnificent owner-bred colt Crepello added the Derby to his Two Thousand Guineas victory. There now seems nothing to stop him becoming the first Triple Crown winner since Bahram twenty-two-years ago.' He added that Lester 'rode him with unbelievable confidence and exemplary polish', and the jockey's performance received as much attention as the horse's. John Rickman in the *Daily Mail* declared the race 'the roughest Derby I have ever seen' but judged Lester's ride 'superlative'. Clive Graham in the *Daily Express* described his handling of the favourite as 'impeccable', while Graham's colleague Peter O'Sullevan wryly noted that 'calm, pale Lester Piggott has survived the only ordeal he regarded with any apprehension, "the press interviews after the race".' At one of those interviews Lester was asked how he would celebrate the win. He replied: 'I shall spend a quiet evening. When I won the Derby on Never Say Die I went home and cut the lawn. I haven't cut the lawn since.'

*   *   *

Sadly Crepello never ran again. He was considered a certainty for the St Leger at Doncaster in September, where victory would make him the first winner of the Triple Crown since 1935. But there were other big prizes to be won, and following the Derby his next target was the King George VI and Queen Elizabeth Stakes at Ascot in July, still in its infancy but already the top all-aged middle-distance race run in Britain. Noel Murless had made it clear that Crepello would not be suited by heavy ground and would not run in the race were the going to come up too soft, but in the days before the race there seemed little prospect of that, and Crepello scared off most of the serious opposition. The night before the race the heavens opened, and the rain continued to fall throughout the morning, with the result that Crepello was withdrawn. This unleashed a barrage of criticism on Noel's head but he was unrepentant: the horse would not be risked in bad going. The priority was to win the St Leger and thus the Triple Crown, and there would always be next year for Crepello to win the King George. The fact that the 1957 King George was won by Montaval, who had been beaten in the Eclipse Stakes by Arctic Explorer, a Murless colt not remotely in the same league as Crepello at home, showed that the Derby winner would certainly have won at Ascot. But Noel was adamant that Crepello should not run, and that was that.

Crepello was then trained for the St Leger in September and all seemed to be going well. No three-year-old colt could hold a candle to him, and he was a certainty. Then in early August he finished lame after a routine gallop at Newmarket: he had broken down on one of his forelegs, and would never race again. This news stunned the racing world, but in all honesty it did not come as a complete surprise to me. A heavy-topped horse like Crepello would always be difficult to train,

and he had done wonderfully well to win the Two Thousand Guineas over a distance much too short for him, and then the Derby over a course for which he was not by any means ideally built.

How good was Crepello? He was never given the opportunity to prove his worth by competing against horses from a different generation, and on that account it is difficult to weigh him up with any confidence. All I know is that on Derby Day 1957 he was brilliant, certainly in the same league as Sir Ivor and Nijinsky later in my career. Form experts can point to the subsequent achievements of Ballymoss to underline Crepello's greatness, but what really counts is how he felt on the day, and to me he felt as good as any Derby winner. I have no doubt that, had his legs stood training, he would have proved himself one of the all-time greats.

Lester's two Classic winners within three days in June 1957: on the right, Crepello; on the left, the Queen's filly Carrozza, winner of the Oaks.

* * *

Crepello stood as a stallion at Sir Victor Sassoon's Beech House Stud in Newmarket, and his offspring included many top-class horses. His son Busted won the Eclipse Stakes and King George VI and Queen Elizabeth

Lester and Crepello.

Stakes in 1967, and he was also the sire of several notable fillies: Caergwrle, winner of the One Thousand Guineas in 1968, Celina (Irish Oaks 1968), Lucyrowe (Coronation Stakes and Nassau Stakes, 1969), Crepellana (Prix de Diane, 1969) and Mysterious (1973 One Thousand Guineas, Oaks and Yorkshire Oaks). He was leading sire in 1969.

Crepello died at the age of twenty in October 1974, not long after his grandson Bustino, a son of Busted, had won the St Leger.

Crepello

Pedigree

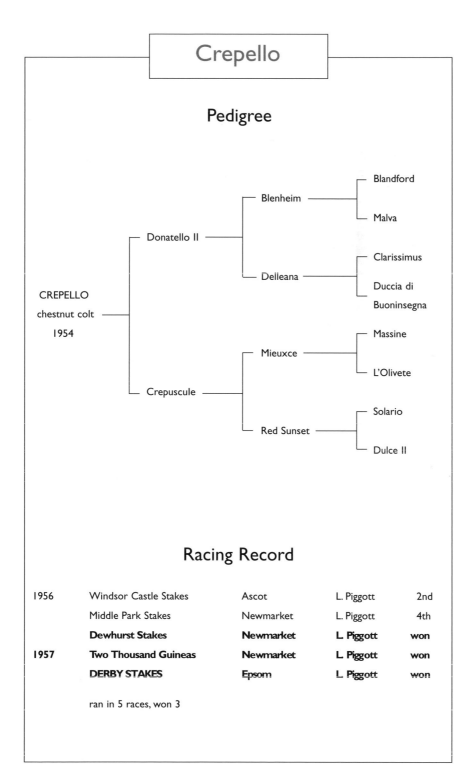

CREPELLO
chestnut colt
1954

- Donatello II
  - Blenheim
    - Blandford
    - Malva
  - Delleana
    - Clarissimus
    - Duccia di Buoninsegna
- Crepuscule
  - Mieuxce
    - Massine
    - L'Olivete
  - Red Sunset
    - Solario
    - Dulce II

Racing Record

1956	Windsor Castle Stakes	Ascot	L. Piggott	2nd
	Middle Park Stakes	Newmarket	L. Piggott	4th
	Dewhurst Stakes	**Newmarket**	**L. Piggott**	**won**
1957	**Two Thousand Guineas**	**Newmarket**	**L. Piggott**	**won**
	DERBY STAKES	**Epsom**	**L. Piggott**	**won**

ran in 5 races, won 3

1960
ST PADDY

Previous pages:
St Paddy and Lester.

181st Derby Stakes

1 June 1960
going: firm
£33,052 to winner

1	**ST PADDY**	**L. Piggott**	**7–1**
2	ALCAEUS	A. Breasley	10–1
3	KYTHNOS	R. Hutchinson	7–1
4	AUROY	G. Lewis	33–1
5	Proud Chieftain	S. Clayton	66–1
6	Die Hard	G. Bougoure	9–2
7	Tulyartos	W. Williamson	7–1
8	Marengo	R. Fawdon	9–1
9	Tudor Period	W. Rickaby	66–1
10	Oak Ridge	E. Hide	66–1
11	Lustrous Hope	G. Moore	28–1
12	Ides Of March	E. Eldin	50–1
13	Chrysler III	J. Mercer	45–1
14	Mr Higgins	D. Smith	50–1
15	Port St Anne	S. Millbanks	200–1
16	Picture Goer	W. Elliott	200–1
fell	Angers	G. Thiboeuf	2–1 fav

17 ran
distances: 3 lengths, ½ length
time: 2 minutes 35.6 seconds
Winner owned and bred by Sir Victor Sassoon,
trained at Newmarket by Noel Murless

Just three years after Crepello, another colt owned by Sir Victor Sassoon, trained by Noel Murless and ridden by Lester Piggott swept to an easy success in the Derby. St Paddy's victory in 1960 followed two more Derby losers for Lester. In 1958 Boccaccio, trained by Noel Murless, started at 20–1 after finishing fifth behind Bald Eagle in the Dante Stakes at York. In the Derby he failed to make much impression, finishing well beaten behind fifty-one-year-old Charlie Smirke on Sir Victor's third Derby winner in six runnings – Hard Ridden, trained in Ireland by Mickey Rogers.

The following year Lester rode Murless-trained Carnoustie, who appeared to have a reasonable chance, having finished third to Taboun in the Two Thousand Guineas after winning the Classic Trial at Thirsk. Carnoustie started at 10–1 at Epsom for what appeared a very open Derby, but could finish only sixth behind Parthia.

St Paddy, a bay son of Aureole, runner-up in the Queen's colours behind Pinza in 1953, had a much more obvious chance than either Boccaccio or Carnoustie. As a two-year-old he had run only twice. After showing plenty of promise on the home gallops he started favourite against some much more exposed rivals in the Acomb Stakes over six furlongs at the York August meeting, but was less than fully wound up for his racecourse debut, and in the circumstances ran encouragingly, though unplaced behind the winner Beau Ideal. He then went for the prestigious Royal Lodge Stakes at the Ascot September meeting. Starting co-favourite with Goose Creek and Jet Stream, he turned in an extremely polished performance for such an inexperienced colt, taking up the running early in the straight and forging clear to win unchallenged by five lengths. This highly impressive performance led the Murless camp to entertain serious Classic hopes.

But the month before the 1960 season began there was a more pressing matter for Lester than any big-race ride, and on 22 February he married Susan Armstrong, daughter of trainer Sam Armstrong. Like Lester, she had ridden racehorses at a very early age – her father had moved to Newmarket from Middleham in Yorkshire after the war – and she was a horsewoman of note. In 1958 she had been narrowly beaten by Noel Murless's daughter Julie in the Newmarket Town Plate (in those days the only race open to lady riders, and an event she won twice), and the

Piggotts' first Newmarket house was named Florizel (as is their present house) after the horse she rode that day.

*　*　*

Of all my Derby winners, St Paddy has probably been the least well served by later assessments, and he never really got the credit he deserved. On his day he was a very good colt indeed, though he had one serious fault: he pulled very hard, and for a long while it was almost impossible to settle him in a race. At York for his two-year-old debut he bolted on the way to the start – hardly the ideal preparation for his first ever race – and in the circumstances I was pleased that he ran as well as he did, as a horse who has bolted can never have enough energy left for the race itself. After that we fitted him with a gag, a bit designed to restrain a head-strong horse, and he was much more amenable in the Royal Lodge Stakes. He was tremendously impressive that day.

He wintered well, and for his first race in 1960 was aimed at the Two Thousand Guineas at Newmarket. We did not, in all honesty, expect him to win, as he did not appear to be blessed with instant acceleration and his breeding strongly suggested that he would be more effective at distances longer than a mile. His main target for the season was certainly the Derby, but with the exception of the French-trained Venture VII, who had won the Prix Djebel at Maisons-Laffitte, the field for the Two Thousand Guineas did not look very strong, so it was worth taking our chance. Venture VII started hot favourite at 6–4, with St Paddy second favourite at 5–1.

St Paddy ran very well. Two furlongs out I moved him towards the head of the field, but once he was overtaken by speedier horses like Venture VII and the eventual winner Martial, trained in Ireland by Paddy Prendergast, St Paddy had very little response, and with the Derby only five weeks away I was not hard on him. We finished sixth, and for me that was a perfectly satisfactory Derby trial.

Crepello had gone straight to the Derby from the Guineas, but St Paddy was a colt with significantly less experience, so it was decided to give him another race – only the fourth of his life – before Epsom. The ideal race was the Dante Stakes, run over ten and a half furlongs at York two weeks before the Derby. St Paddy had much the best overall form of the ten runners and started odds on. As a counter to his inclination to pull, he wore a special restraining noseband when going down, though once at the start it was removed, and like most of Noel Murless's horses he raced in a bridle without any noseband. St Paddy absolutely cruised home in the Dante, taking the lead a furlong out and strolling home without coming out of a canter to win by three lengths from Ancient Lights.

All looked set fair for Epsom. St Paddy had the best form of any home-trained staying three-year-old, but there was a stiff overseas challenge. At that time the French always sent a powerful team over for the Derby – Phil Drake had won in 1955 and Lavandin in 1956 – and in 1960 their best hope lay with Angers, trained by George Bridgland. He had won the Prix Jean Prat and Prix Hocquart – both at Longchamp – very easily and clearly had a serious chance in the Derby. From Ireland came Die Hard, a son of Never Say Die unbeaten in three races earlier in 1960 (he had not run as a two-year-old). On Derby Day, Die Hard was officially described as being trained by Phonsie O'Brien, Vincent's brother, as the previous month Vincent himself had had his training licence taken away by the Irish racing authorities: a horse of his named Chamour had been alleged to have a minute amount of stimulant in his system when winning a maiden race at The Curragh in April 1960, and though Vincent protested his innocence and the Irish racing public was up in arms, the ban lasted a year and Die Hard – owned, like Ballymoss, by the American John McShain, head of the construction company which had built the Pentagon – was officially trained by his brother.

Angers started a warm favourite for the Derby at 2–1, with Die Hard 9–2 and St Paddy co-third favourite at 7–1 with two other Irish challengers: Kythnos, trained by Paddy Prendergast, had won the Irish Two Thousand Guineas, and Tulyartos, trained by Seamus McGrath, was a son of Tulyar and had run fourth in the Two Thousand Guineas at Newmarket.

What a hard-pulling horse needs is a good strong pace which will allow him to stride out in a proper rhythm and not waste valuable

Opposite page:

The finish, 1960:
St Paddy well clear of
Alcaeus (Scobie
Breasley, left) and
Kythnos (Ron
Hutchinson)
on the rail.

energy fighting for his head, and from that point of view the Derby, with a field that year of seventeen runners, was bound to be run to suit St Paddy. A Derby field never dawdles, and while you hear plenty of excuses after every running, lack of pace is never one of them.

From my point of view the race went perfectly. St Paddy took the preliminaries well, arrived at the start on good terms with himself, and in the race itself was always travelling very easily. For the first half mile he ran about fifth or sixth as Die Hard took the field along with the rank outsiders Tudor Period (ridden by my cousin Bill Rickaby) and Port St Anne. Early on the run down the hill the favourite Angers fell, though he was towards the rear of the field at the time and I was not aware that anything untoward had happened.

I manoeuvred St Paddy towards the inside as we made a forward move, and by Tattenham Corner had the perfect position: Die Hard still led, with Auroy and Tulyartos chasing him and St Paddy going very well within himself on the inside. Three furlongs out I decided it was time to go on in earnest: St Paddy took the lead with a quarter of a mile to go and then galloped on relentlessly, without ever looking in the slightest danger of getting caught. I never asked him a serious question, yet he won with complete ease. Alcaeus, ridden by Scobie Breasley (the great Australian rider who had been champion jockey three years earlier but had not yet won the Derby), ran on to finish second, three lengths behind us, while Kythnos plugged on at one pace to finish third. Die Hard was sixth. I later learned that Angers had broken a leg and had been destroyed: whether he would have given St Paddy a fight we can't know, but it was a sad postscript to the race.

* * *

Even before the race, the 1960 Derby had already been touched by tragedy, as the Irish runner Exchange Student had broken a leg exercising on the Downs the day before and had been put down, so it is perhaps not surprising that press coverage of the death of Angers rubbed a good deal of the gloss off a tremendous performance from St Paddy. John Rickman in the *Daily Mail* reported Scobie Breasley's claim that he would have won on Alcaeus had the horse not been interfered with when Angers fell, then

added: 'You must balance against this the fact that St Paddy won very comfortably.' Rickman went on to repeat Lester's claim that he had never won the Derby more easily.

Lester's third Derby was Noel Murless's second, after Crepello in 1957, and Sir Victor Sassoon's fourth in eight runnings, after Pinza in 1953, Crepello in 1957 and Hard Ridden in 1958: he had had to wait a long time to achieve his ambition, but then to enjoy such a concentration of success was remarkable.

For all the ease of his victory, the position of St Paddy in any ranking of Lester's Derby winners is undermined by the subsequent performances of the horses he beat, few of whom achieved much afterwards. Alcaeus was beaten in the Irish Derby, though Tulyartos ran second to Javelot in the Eclipse Stakes and Kythnos was third behind Aggressor and the filly Petite Etoile – one of the greatest horses Lester ever rode – in the King George VI and Queen Elizabeth Stakes.

St Paddy coming back, preceded by a relieved-looking Noel Murless.

A few days after that controversial King George – in which Lester on Petite Etoile failed to peg back Jimmy Lindley on the outsider Aggressor – St Paddy made his first appearance since the Derby, in the Gordon Stakes at Goodwood.

The Derby had left St Paddy a little jarred up, so Noel Murless decided to give him a break from the rigours of training before building him up towards the St Leger in September. He had also been coughing after the Derby and was well short of peak fitness in the Gordon Stakes at Goodwood at the end of July, some two months after Epsom: I was not surprised that after taking the lead with a quarter of a mile to go he blew up inside the final furlong, allowing us to be caught close home by Kipling and beaten half a length. It would have been stupid to subject him to a hard race with more important targets to come, and next time out in the Great Voltigeur Stakes at York in August he quickened well close home to win narrowly from Apostle. So he went to Doncaster for the St Leger in the best of shape, mentally and physically, and turned in a superb performance. After being held up while his stable companion Off Key made the pace, St Paddy strode to the front three furlongs out and galloped on resolutely. Inside the final furlong he was all of five lengths clear, and I eased him down to win by three lengths from Die Hard and Sir Winston Churchill's good colt Vienna (who had been forced to miss the Derby due to the blacksmith pricking the sole of his foot when shoeing him before the race). There were still plenty who carped about the value of St Paddy's form, and he had never raced against older horses, but in the Derby and St Leger he was a very good three-year-old indeed.

St Paddy was the first of my Derby winners to be kept in training as a four-year-old – and, following 1959 winner Parthia, the second successive Derby winner to race at four at a time when it was very much the exception rather than the rule – and we had high hopes of him in 1961. His first race of the campaign, when he beat two inferior opponents (one of them his own pacemaker Sunny Way) in the Coombe Stakes at Sandown Park in May, told us very little, but he then won the Hardwicke

Stakes at Royal Ascot in a canter from Vienna and Die Hard (to whom he was conceding ten pounds and six pounds respectively).

Next stop Sandown Park for the Eclipse Stakes, usually billed as the first big middle-distance race of the season when the Classic generation take on their elders. The 1961 renewal had just seven runners and a very one-sided look, with St Paddy starting 2–13 favourite and Pinzon, supposedly the best of the three-year-olds after showing some decent but far from top-class form earlier in the season, second favourite at 100–9. This time the services of Sunny Way as pacemaker were dispensed with, and St Paddy was allowed to make his own running, which he did in relentless fashion. Not for a moment did I worry that we would be caught, and by the home turn all the others were struggling. Without ever coming off the bit, St Paddy won by a length and a half from Proud Chieftain, with Blast third and Right Of Way fourth. Pinzon, best of the trio of three-year-olds, was a remote fifth. That Eclipse was hardly a true 'Clash of the Generations', but it is a mark of St Paddy's quality that he broke the Sandown Park track record for ten furlongs that day.

In his next race St Paddy did meet a top-notch three-year-old in the shape of Right Royal V. Trained in France by Etienne Pollet, Right Royal V had earlier in 1961 easily won both the Poule d'Essai des Poulains and the Prix du Jockey-Club – French equivalents of the Two Thousand Guineas and Derby – and in between these two races the hardly less prestigious Prix Lupin. He was clearly out of the very top drawer, but so was St Paddy, and the pair were vastly superior to their two opponents in what was then the smallest ever field for the King George, as the betting reflected: 4–5 St Paddy, 6–4 Right Royal, 20–1 Apostle, whom St Paddy had beaten as a three-year-old, and Rockavon, shock winner of the 1961 Two Thousand Guineas.

As in the Eclipse, I tried to make all the running on St Paddy, and at the turn into the short Ascot straight thought I might have had Right Royal's measure, but a furlong and a half out the French colt came up alongside us, then went away quite easily to win by three lengths. Although I knew the soft ground was not to St Paddy's liking, I had hoped for better.

Soon after the King George came the news that St Paddy's owner Sir Victor Sassoon, who had suffered a heart attack not long before, had died. This cast a great gloom over Warren Place, as his horses were such a central part of the operation there. He had always been very generous to me – I have already mentioned the gift of the Lincoln Continental after Crepello's Derby – and I won many big races in his colours, not only with Crepello and St Paddy but with many other horses including Twilight Alley: by the time that giant of a horse won the Ascot Gold Cup in 1963 the famous colours had been taken over by Lady Sassoon.

Plans to run St Paddy in the Vaux Gold Tankard at Redcar or Ebor Handicap at York – to run a Derby winner in any handicap, however valuable, would be unthinkable today – were dropped when he suffered minor setbacks, and his next race was the Jockey Club Stakes over a mile and three quarters at Newmarket at the end of September, a race run over the round Sefton Course, discontinued after the 1973 season. St Paddy won this from another of Sir Winston Churchill's good horses, High Hat, and returned to Newmarket for the Champion Stakes over the straight ten furlongs the following month. He started odds-on and appeared to be cruising home in the final furlong when Proud Chieftain and the French colt Bobar II both came at him with vigorous challenges. I called for an extra effort, but St Paddy had gone very flat: Bobar II headed us close home and won by three quarters of a length. Some said that the Champion Stakes was too short for St Paddy, but Proud Chieftain, whom we had beaten easily in the Eclipse (also over ten furlongs) when giving him seven pounds and whom we now met at level weights, was just a length behind us at Newmarket, so that cannot have been St Paddy's true running.

Sadly he did not have a chance to redeem his reputation, as the Champion Stakes turned out to have been his last race.

Once he had learned not to pull all the time, St Paddy was a magnificent racehorse – beautifully proportioned and blessed with a tremendous gallop. His defeat by Right Royal V at Ascot rather tarnished his reputation, but on his day – and there were a good few of those, including the 1960 Derby – he was outstanding.

* * *

St Paddy won £101,527 in win and place prize money, a huge total for the time: indeed, his aggregate of win prize money was second only to that of

Following pages:
St Paddy at Beech House Stud, Newmarket, 1969.

Ballymoss in the record of all-time money-earners. None of his offspring won an English Classic, though his son Connaught ran second in the 1968 Derby to Sir Ivor (ridden by Lester: see pages 78–99 below) and went on to win the 1970 Eclipse Stakes, and his daughter St Pauli Girl was runner-up in both One Thousand Guineas and Oaks in 1967. Arguably his best son was Parnell, winner of the Irish St Leger in 1971 and the following year a close second to Brigadier Gerard in the King George at Ascot. Another of his sons was Patch, short-head runner-up in the 1975 Prix du Jockey-Club. St Paddy retired from stud duties in 1981, and was put down in 1984 at the age of twenty-seven.

St Paddy's Derby was one of 170 winners ridden by Lester in the 1960 season, enough to make him champion jockey for the first time. The only other jockeys to top 100 winners that term were Scobie Breasley (153), Doug Smith (144) and Joe Sime (108).

Three winners from seven Derby rides between 1954 and 1960 had made Lester the outstanding Derby jockey of his generation by the age of twenty-four, but after St Paddy he missed the next two renewals of the race. The Derbys of 1961 and 1962 are emphatically not on the list of Lester's best racing memories.

The 1961 season dawned with the Murless yard seemingly having every prospect of adding a third Piggott-ridden Derby winner in the colours of Sir Victor Sassoon. Pinturischio was a son of Sir Victor's 1953 winner Pinza, and a finely built, imposing colt. He had not run as a two-year-old, having spent a good part of the 1960 season suffering from a cough, and was not put into serious training until August that year. Despite never having run in a race, Pinturischio gradually built a huge reputation on the strength of his work on the Newmarket gallops, and throughout the winter was a strong favourite for both the Two Thousand Guineas and Derby.

Rarely has a racecourse debut been as keenly awaited as that of Pinturischio in the Wood Ditton Stakes at Newmarket on 13 April 1961. It was an open secret that not long before he had worked exceptionally well against a fellow Murless three-year-old Aurelius, and when that colt won the Craven Stakes two days before the Wood Ditton, defeat for his stable companion seemed even more unlikely (and would have been completely out of the question had anyone then known that Aurelius would go on to win the 1961 St Leger, ridden by Lester).

Pinturischio started at 2–5 for his first race and never gave his backers the slightest cause for concern, winning in a canter from six opponents.

This debut effort thrust Pinturischio even more prominently into the foreground of the Classic picture, and back at Newmarket a fortnight later he started a very warm 7–4 favourite for the Two Thousand Guineas, with the Paddy Prendergast-trained Typhoon at 6–1 the only other runner starting at single-figure odds. In a finish dominated by outsiders, 66–1 chance Rockavon won well from another 66–1 shot Prince Tudor, with Time Greine (25–1) a short head back in third. Pinturischio, who had become unbalanced when mounting his challenge a furlong out, was fourth, and a 50–1 chance named Psidium (of whom the official form book's only comment was 'sweating') finished way behind. Lester was not as downcast as he might have been by Pinturischio's effort: 'Although disappointed', he wrote later, 'I was convinced that the race had brought him on a great deal, and was still certain that over a mile and a half at Epsom he would prove very hard to beat.'

Sadly Lester was never able to find out whether he was right. After the Guineas it was announced that Pinturischio would run in the Dante Stakes at York to give him more experience before the Derby, then the week before the race came news that he would miss York on account of a high temperature — soon accepted as a euphemism for the colt having been doped so that he would miss the Derby: Pinturischio had been the only horse seriously backed in the ante-post market, and thus a good many people stood to benefit from his non-appearance at Epsom. Tim Fitzgeorge-Parker's biography of Noel Murless, *The Guv'nor*, quotes the trainer: 'I was warned a few days beforehand that he would be nobbled, but didn't think that anything would happen until the horse had run in the Dante Stakes … Later some woman wrote an article in one of the Sunday papers saying that they had sat up in the big tree at the back of the yard and waited until everything was closed up at night and that they then got in through the skylight in Pinturischio's box. Of course they did not get in through the skylight. They just picked the locks on the door. Then they gave him a very strong physic, the stuff, I believe, that they give to elephants. It must have been terribly powerful. He was never the same horse again and although for a short while I hoped that I would be able to get him right again to run in

the Derby, they broke in a second time and made no mistake. They really finished him off.' Poor Pinturischio was scratched from the Derby four days before the race, never ran again, and remains one of the most inglorious footnotes in British racing history.

Pinturischio's late defection left Lester without a ride in the 1961 Derby. He had, however, been made an offer earlier in the year. Three days after the Wood Ditton Stakes he had ridden a colt named Psidium to finish fourth in the Prix Daru over ten and a half furlongs at Longchamp. Moutiers, who won that race, became a leading fancy for the Derby, and when Psidium's trainer Harry Wragg (who had himself ridden three Derby winners) later approached Lester about riding his horse at Epsom, the offer was politely declined. For one thing, Lester was at that stage committed to riding Pinturischio; for another, he was convinced by his Longchamp running that Psidium would not stay the Derby distance – 'He wouldn't get a mile and a half in a horse box', he was quoted as saying – and in any case, how could he possibly beat Moutiers?

So for once the Derby fates conspired against Lester, who had no rides at Epsom on Derby Day and sat at home in Newmarket watching on television as Psidium, ridden by the French jockey Roger Poincelet, came from last of the twenty-eight runners at the top of the hill to win the Derby by two lengths at 66–1. Lester's reaction was characteristic: 'These things happen.'

(Peter O'Sullevan had written in his Derby preview in the *Daily Express* that he would be 'psurprised' if Psidium won, and after the race was approached by the colt's owner Etty Plesch, who asked, 'What are you going to say now?' O'Sullevan's answer: 'Consider me in psackcloth.')

In 1962 Lester's expected Derby ride was Young Lochinvar, in the Sassoon colours now registered to Sir Victor's widow. Having finished unplaced in the Blue Riband Trial Stakes at Epsom and then runner-up in the Chester Vase, Young Lochinvar did not appear to have a major chance, but any prospect Lester had of a fourth Derby was dashed by the outcome of a selling plate at the evening meeting at Lincoln a week before the big race. Lester rode a filly named Ione for the small Staffordshire trainer Bob Ward, and finished runner-up to the other Ward runner Polly Macaw. The racecourse stewards suspected foul play – Ione had drifted in the betting from 4–6 to 11–8 while Polly Macaw had shortened from 3–1 to evens – and when the case was referred to the Stewards of the Jockey Club, Lester, despite protesting his innocence, found himself with a two-month suspension which involved missing not only the Derby but also Royal Ascot, the Irish Derby, the Newmarket July Meeting and the King George. For the second year running he was forced to watch the Derby on television at home. Larkspur – on whom earlier that season he had finished unplaced in the Madrid Free Handicap at The Curragh – won to give Vincent O'Brien his first Derby, but the race was marred by no fewer than seven horses falling on the run down the hill. Young Lochinvar, ridden by Willie Snaith, finished well back.

Normal service was resumed in 1963, when Lester's Derby ride was Corpora, trained in France by Ernie Fellows. Corpora, a son of the great Italian horse Ribot, had run third behind Only For Life in the Two Thousand Guineas and at Epsom started fourth favourite at 100–8. He was close behind the leaders at Tattenham Corner, but then could only plug on at one pace and finished fifth, just over ten lengths behind the winner Relko.

In 1964 Lester was back in the Sassoon colours to ride Sweet Moss, who came to Epsom in good form, having won the Dee Stakes at Chester and the Dante Stakes at York. Like Corpora he started at 100–8, but failed to make any impression on the race and finished well back behind Santa Claus, a first Derby winner – at the age of fifty – for Lester's great riding rival of the 1960s, Scobie Breasley. (Fourth in that race was 100–1 chance Anselmo, the one and only Derby runner trained by Lester's father Keith, who had bought the colt for the pop singer Billy Fury.)

In 1965 Lester rode Meadow Court for Irish trainer Paddy Prendergast. In any normal year Meadow Court would have been hailed as a top-class Derby winner, but this was no normal year, as the twenty-two-runner field

Cue for a song: Bing Crosby greets Lester and Meadow Court after the 1965 Irish Derby. Trainer Paddy Prendergast is behind Meadow Court, in the trilby hat.

included Sea Bird II. Though he had been beaten once as a two-year-old in his native France, Sea Bird II boasted some top-class form before the Derby and started 7–4 favourite, with Meadow Court, who in his most recent race had been runner-up in the Dante Stakes, second favourite at 10–1. Lester rode Meadow Court in his trademark Derby way, with the colt perfectly positioned just behind the leaders at Tattenham Corner, but once Pat Glennon and Sea Bird II had sauntered to the front approaching the final furlong the race was over. Meadow Court ran on well and finished two lengths behind the winner, but Sea Bird II had turned in perhaps the greatest Derby performance of all time, and there was no answer to his brilliance.

By the time the two horses met again in the Prix de l'Arc de Triomphe at Longchamp in October, Meadow Court had proved himself a colt of the highest class, winning the Irish Derby (after which his co-owner Bing Crosby launched into an impromptu rendition of 'When Irish Eyes Are Smiling', to the great delight of the Curragh crowd) and the King George VI and Queen Elizabeth Stakes, though he was beaten by ten lengths by Provoke in the St Leger, run in desperate going. Although Meadow Court ran unplaced in the Arc as Sea Bird II galloped into Turf immortality by winning by six lengths despite veering diagonally across the wide Longchamp straight, he could be regarded as Lester's best Derby ride not to win the race: at Epsom on 2 June 1965 he simply came up against a freak of nature.

In 1966 Lester rode Right Noble, 9–2 joint favourite for the Derby. Right Noble's physique did not please everyone – Derby historian Roger Mortimer wrote that he 'would not have looked grotesquely out of place with a trombonist on his back in the Household Cavalry Mounted Band' – and had failed to win in three races as a two-year-old, but his performance when scoring a facile victory in the White Rose Stakes at Ascot at the end of April (beating the subsequent St Leger winner Sodium into third) made him a leading fancy for the Derby. On the day he shared top spot in the betting market with subsequent runner-up Pretendre, who had won the Blue Riband Trial Stakes at Epsom earlier in the season.

Although he finished unplaced at Epsom behind Charlottown (a second Derby winner for Scobie Breasley, then aged fifty-two), Right Noble has a significant place in Lester Piggott's Derby history, as the colt was the first of nine Derby runners he rode for Irish trainer Vincent O'Brien.

Born in County Cork in 1917, Michael Vincent O'Brien bred and trained greyhounds before taking in the first horses at his yard at Churchtown, sending out his first winner in May 1943. By the late 1940s he was one of the leading National Hunt trainers in Ireland, his most famous charge at that time being the great chaser Cottage Rake, winner of three consecutive Cheltenham Gold Cups in 1948, 1949 and 1950; O'Brien won a fourth Gold Cup with Knock Hard in 1953. Among his many other stellar achievements as a jumps trainer are three consecutive Champion Hurdles with Hatton's Grace in 1949, 1950 and 1951, and – perhaps most remarkable of all – winning the Grand National three years running with three different horses: Early Mist in 1953, Royal Tan in 1954 and Quare Times in 1955. By then he had moved his training base to Ballydoyle, near Cashel in County Tipperary. Initially he had to make gaps in the hedges to accommodate the gallops, but he gradually built up Ballydoyle to the point where the very word was synonymous with the absolute best in racehorse training, a world-famous establishment where no detail was too small to be over-looked. Among many other innovations, O'Brien built his own landing strip for transporting his horses to England and France by plane and installed electrical equipment for timing the gallops, and of particular relevance to his Derby record is the building of a left-hand bend similar to Tattenham Corner, over which his Derby hopes would be worked to assess how well they might handle the real thing at Epsom.

* * *

I first met Vincent O'Brien at Cheltenham races in the late 1950s, when he was beginning to wind down his involvement with National Hunt in favour of the Flat, and first rode for him when the great mare Gladness won the 1958 Ascot Gold Cup: she followed up in the Goodwood Cup and Ebor Handicap the same year. Over the next few years I rode for him on and off – including riding a race on Larkspur early in 1962, though riding him in the Derby was out of the question as I was committed to Noel Murless – but riding for him in 1966 caused all sorts of fallout.

Right Noble was owned by the American industrialist Charles Engelhard, who had horses in training with Vincent in Ireland and with Fulke Johnson Houghton in England. Vincent asked me to ride the colt at Ascot, and after he had won so easily there offered me the ride for the Derby. Noel Murless had no obvious Derby candidate that year, so I agreed. The trouble started when Vincent asked if I could also ride his filly Valoris in the Oaks. She had won the Irish One Thousand Guineas very easily and looked a good thing for the fillies' Classic at Epsom, but Noel had what he considered a very live Oaks candidate in Varinia, whom I had ridden when runner-up in the Cheshire Oaks before (ridden by Stan Clayton) she had won the Oaks Trial at Lingfield. As far as I was concerned Valoris was a certainty for the Oaks, and I told Noel – with whom, that season, I had an informal agreement but not a formal contract, as I was riding more and more for overseas trainers and wanted a degree of freedom in making my riding plans – that I would ride Vincent's filly rather than his. Understandably enough Noel took a dim view of this, and as the row rumbled on even the Jockey Club got involved. But since there was no agreement there could have been no breach, and while I was sad to leave Noel after twelve years at Warren Place, I never thought I was doing the wrong thing.

Right Noble was not really built for Epsom and failed to act on the track, but Valoris duly won the Oaks very easily, with Varinia (again ridden by Stan Clayton) well beaten in third.

* * *

Lester further cemented the new relationship with Vincent O'Brien in July 1966 when winning the Eclipse Stakes on Pieces Of Eight, and the following week proved that bridges with Noel Murless had not been burned when landing the King George VI and Queen Elizabeth Stakes at Ascot on the Warren Place-trained filly Aunt Edith. Later in the season he partnered Murless's highly promising two-year-old Royal Palace to win the Acomb Stakes at York and Royal Lodge Stakes at Ascot and become a leading candidate for the Derby the following year.

The 1967 Derby was the first to be started from starting stalls, which had been introduced to British racing two years previously. (The first race started from stalls, the Chesterfield Stakes at Newmarket in July 1965, was won by

Lester on Track Spare.) Lester again donned the Charles Engelhard silks to ride Ribocco, trained in Berkshire by Fulke Johnson Houghton. Ribocco had won three of his four races as a two-year-old – notably the Observer Gold Cup (now the Racing Post Trophy) at Doncaster – but his three runs in 1967 before the Derby all proved disappointing: fourth in the Craven Stakes and second when odds-on in the Dee Stakes (ridden in both by Lester), then unplaced in the Lingfield Derby Trial (ridden by Ron Hutchinson). So bad was the Lingfield run that he was taken out of ante-post lists as there seemed no way he could run in the Derby: he simply was failing to make normal improvement, and, as with a good many sons of Ribot, his temperament was suspect. Meanwhile Lester had been offered the Derby ride on the Murless-trained Sun Rock, the Warren Place second string behind Royal Palace, who had won the Two Thousand Guineas and was a very hot favourite for Epsom, where he would be ridden by the Australian jockey George Moore. With Ribocco seemingly a non-runner Lester agreed to ride Sun Rock, but then Sun Rock was withdrawn, and word came that Ribocco was thriving again and would run after all. Lester would ride.

Ribocco disliked being bustled in his races and hitting him with the whip was out of the question, so Lester had to nurse him along towards the rear of the field and keep him close to the outside until, once into the straight, he brought him with a sweeping run up the wide outside as Royal Palace set sail for home. Ribocco ran on strongly but Royal Palace was far too good, winning by two and a half lengths. Dart Board was third, two lengths behind Ribocco.

Any regrets that Lester might have harboured about seeing three of the first four Classics of 1967 won by Murless-trained horses ridden by George Moore – Fleet had won the One Thousand Guineas in addition to Royal Palace's Two Thousand Guineas and Derby – were soon assuaged by Ribocco's post-Derby form: he won the Irish Derby, ran third to the Murless-trained Busted in the King George, easily won the St Leger (which Royal Palace was forced to miss due to injury), and was narrowly beaten into third place in the Prix de l'Arc de Triomphe, only a neck and a short head behind he winner Topyo. Ribocco then ran unplaced in the Washington DC International at Laurel Park in Maryland, and was retired to stud.

St Paddy

Pedigree

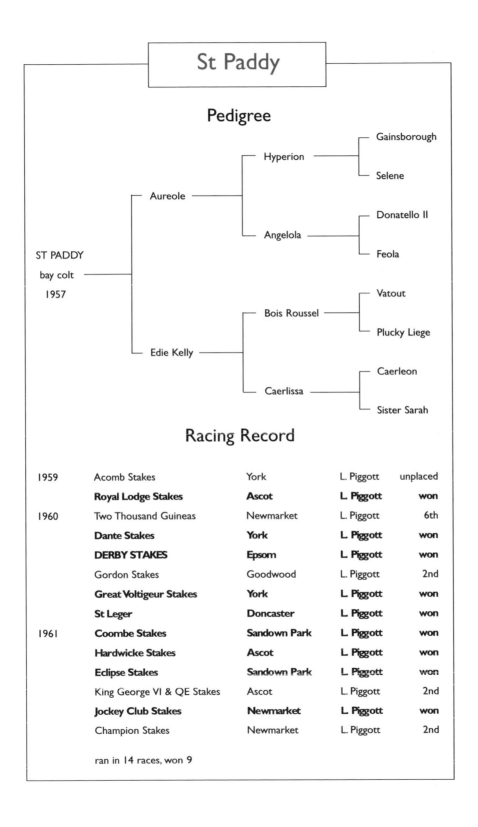

ST PADDY
bay colt
1957

- Aureole
  - Hyperion
    - Gainsborough
    - Selene
  - Angelola
    - Donatello II
    - Feola
- Edie Kelly
  - Bois Roussel
    - Vatout
    - Plucky Liege
  - Caerlissa
    - Caerleon
    - Sister Sarah

Racing Record

1959	Acomb Stakes	York	L. Piggott	unplaced
	Royal Lodge Stakes	**Ascot**	**L. Piggott**	**won**
1960	Two Thousand Guineas	Newmarket	L. Piggott	6th
	Dante Stakes	**York**	**L. Piggott**	**won**
	DERBY STAKES	**Epsom**	**L. Piggott**	**won**
	Gordon Stakes	Goodwood	L. Piggott	2nd
	Great Voltigeur Stakes	**York**	**L. Piggott**	**won**
	St Leger	**Doncaster**	**L. Piggott**	**won**
1961	**Coombe Stakes**	**Sandown Park**	**L. Piggott**	**won**
	Hardwicke Stakes	**Ascot**	**L. Piggott**	**won**
	Eclipse Stakes	**Sandown Park**	**L. Piggott**	**won**
	King George VI & QE Stakes	Ascot	L. Piggott	2nd
	Jockey Club Stakes	**Newmarket**	**L. Piggott**	**won**
	Champion Stakes	Newmarket	L. Piggott	2nd

ran in 14 races, won 9

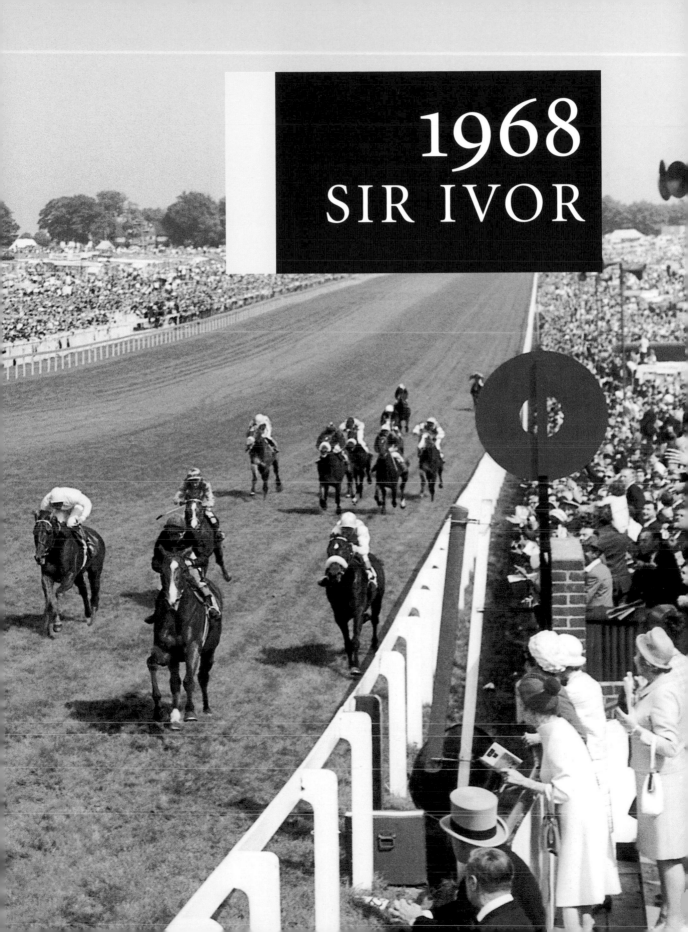

1968
SIR IVOR

Previous pages:
The finish, 1968: Sir Ivor
shoots away from
Connaught (Sandy
Barclay), with Mount
Athos (Ron Hutchinson)
in third place on the rail
and Remand (Joe
Mercer) fourth.

189th Derby Stakes

29 May 1968

going: good

£58,525 10s to winner

1	**SIR IVOR**	L. Piggott	4–5 fav
2	CONNAUGHT	A. Barclay	100–9
3	MOUNT ATHOS	R. Hutchinson	40–1
4	REMAND	J. Mercer	4–1
5	Society	W. Williamson	28–1
6	Torpid	G. Starkey	25–1
7	Atopolis	J. Lindley	40–1
8	Royal Rocket	F. Durr	66–1
9	Myrtus	A. Murray	150–1
10	Floriana	W. Rickaby	200–1
11	Laureate	W. Carson	100–8
12	Benroy	D. Keith	150–1
13	First Rate Pirate	P. Cook	200–1

13 ran

distances 1½ lengths, 2½ lengths

time: 2 minutes 38.7 seconds

Winner bred by Alice Headley Bell, owned by Raymond Guest,
trained at Ballydoyle, County Tipperary, by Vincent O'Brien

Late in 1966 Vincent O'Brien approached the bookmaker William Hill at a party. He wanted to back three of his recently arrived intake of yearlings for the Derby in 1968, and considered 100–1 about each of them a reasonable price. Would Hill accommodate him at those odds?

Unsurprisingly the 1968 Derby, then a year and a half away, had not yet figured in Hill's thinking, but since the three horses concerned were at that point completely unknown quantities, he felt comfortable going along with O'Brien's suggestion, and agreed the price. None of the three colts had yet been named, so O'Brien identified the horses in question to Hill by their breeding. On each of the first two he staked £100, but for the third, a dark bay American-bred colt by Sir Gaylord (whose dam Somethingroyal would later produce the wonder horse Secretariat) out of Attica, he asked for a bet of £500 each way. William Hill agreed to lay the bet. It later transpired that O'Brien had placed that last wager on behalf of Raymond Guest, US Ambassador in Dublin and already owner of one Derby winner, the O'Brien-trained Larkspur in 1962. Soon after the bet had been struck, Guest registered a name for the colt: Sir Ivor.

Sir Ivor had been bought on behalf of Raymond Guest by 'Bull' Hancock, a legend in the bloodstock world, at the yearling sales at Keeneland, Kentucky, for US$42,000 in July 1966. Hancock's prime target at this sale was a colt by the 1948 Two Thousand Guineas winner My Babu, but the bidding had gone way over Guest's limit and Hancock concentrated on acquiring the Sir Gaylord colt. In November that year the colt arrived at O'Brien's stable at Ballydoyle – the first Raymond Guest-owned inmate since Larkspur himself – and the immediate impression he made on the stable staff was not good. His breeder Alice Headley Bell had described him as 'lanky' and 'lopsided' before dispatching him to the sales, and on arrival in Ireland he was so big and backward that there was general pessimism about his running at all as a two-year-old the following year: the horse clearly needed time to develop and mature before being subjected to the rigours of the racecourse.

So it was something of a surprise when Sir Ivor made such progress through the spring of 1967 that he was ready to run in a six-furlong race at The Curragh on Irish Derby day at the beginning of July. Ridden by stable jockey Liam Ward and starting joint favourite, Sir Ivor finished sixth behind Mistigo. Four weeks later he returned to The Curragh to win the

Probationers' Stakes over seven furlongs – this time beating Mistigo at less favourable weights – and in September won the prestigious National Stakes at the same course, in both races ridden, as on his debut, by Liam Ward.

Lester's arrangement with Vincent O'Brien was that he would not ride the stable's horses in Ireland, so it was not until Sir Ivor's fourth race, the Grand Criterium at Longchamp in the middle of October, that one of the most famous partnerships of the jockey's career was launched.

* * *

I had never sat on Sir Ivor before getting the leg-up in the paddock at Longchamp. His first race at The Curragh had been about an hour after I'd won the 1967 Irish Derby on Ribocco, and I knew that there were high hopes for him at Ballydoyle. Then I rode Society to finish third behind him in the National Stakes, and I was very struck by Sir Ivor's turn of foot that day.

My first impression of him at close quarters was of tremendous strength and a wonderful conformation. As a physical specimen he was impossible to fault, and the feeling he gave me going to the start at Longchamp was of a wonderfully balanced and fluid action. The going that day was bottomless – and heavy going at Longchamp is exceptionally testing for a young horse – but Sir Ivor was not troubled by the conditions in the slightest, easing past the leader Pola Bella about a furlong out and cruising home to win by three lengths.

It was a brilliant victory, and one that put the colt bang in the Classic picture for the following season – which presented me with a dilemma.

Life as a freelance jockey after so many years with Noel Murless allowed a great deal of freedom of choice, but it also involved having to make some awkward decisions. Now I had to decide whether to commit myself to riding Sir Ivor in the 1968 Two Thousand Guineas – and, if he came through that race satisfactorily, probably the Derby as well – or go with Petingo, a very high-class colt owned by the Greek shipping magnate Marcos Lemos and trained by my father-in-law Sam Armstrong. Petingo was unbeaten, having won all three of his races as a two-year-old, notably the Gimcrack Stakes at York – by six lengths, with a performance that Timeform said 'almost beggars description' – and the Middle Park Stakes.

Since I had ridden him in all three I knew his qualities at first hand. Petingo topped the Free Handicap for two-year-olds – in those days the official ranking – but Sir Ivor, who did not race in England as a juvenile, was not eligible for a rating. Timeform's *Racehorses of 1967* rated Petingo on 135 and Sir Ivor one pound behind on 134.

Both Sam and Vincent were pressing for a commitment from me before the winter, and eventually I opted to go with Sir Ivor. The deciding factor was that on breeding and on his racing style Petingo was unlikely to stay the mile and a half of the Derby – indeed, I could not see him winning at further than a mile – whereas Sir Ivor's breeding and more relaxed way of running suggested that he had at least a fighting chance of doing so. With the longer term in mind, there was really only one decision to make.

The key to Vincent O'Brien's approach to training racehorses was always to understand the true nature and potential of every horse in his yard and to attend to every detail in order to realise it. In Sir Ivor's case the masterstroke was sending the horse from Ireland in January 1968 to spend the coldest months of the winter in Pisa in order to take advantage of the warmer climate. Despite a scare when Sir Ivor got loose beside a main road and nearly fell into a deep dyke, the colt thrived in the Italian sun, and in March 1968 returned to Ballydoyle a good deal further forward than he would have been had he stayed at home through an Irish winter.

Early in the 1968 season I was booked to ride at Baldoyle, the now defunct racecourse on the coast near Dublin, and while in Ireland I went down to Tipperary to give Sir Ivor a gallop. I could not have been happier with what I saw – Sir Ivor looked magnificent after his time in Italy – or felt: he had developed into a superb three-year-old, just as fluid as the previous year but much stronger. He would clearly take some beating in the Two Thousand Guineas, and gave every expectation of being able to go on from Newmarket to Epsom with a major Derby chance.

The original idea was to open his three-year-old campaign with a run in the Gladness Stakes at The Curragh in March, but Vincent considered him too backward for that race and sent him instead to Ascot for the Two Thousand Guineas Trial in early April. Sir Ivor banged his head on the stalls just as the gates opened, but won handily enough by half a length from Dalry, having taken up the running with over a furlong to go and easing down close home. As we returned to unsaddle I saw that there was blood coming from Sir Ivor's mouth: that bang on the head must have been pretty fierce, and in the circumstances he did well to win as handily as he did.

The Ascot race told me all I wanted to know: Sir Ivor was fit and well and had maintained all of the ability he had showed as a two-year-old.

Sculptor Willie Newton modelled the trophy for the 2002 Vodafone Derby on the famous photograph (opposite page) of Sir Ivor and Lester, both apparently deep in thought, at Epsom on the day before the 1968 Derby.

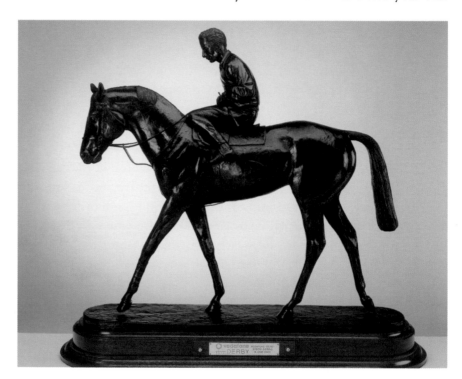

For me, he was a certainty for the Two Thousand Guineas, and I had few worries that I would regret deserting Petingo. At Newmarket, Sir Ivor started warm favourite at 11–8, with Petingo, who had won the Craven Stakes at the course a couple of weeks earlier, at 9–4. My place as Petingo's jockey had been taken by Joe Mercer, but not even when Joe set sail for home going into The Dip did I think for a moment that I had made the wrong decision. Once I asked Sir Ivor to quicken up and go on, he did so effortlessly and won by a length and a half.

Next stop Epsom.

That year's Derby seemed to boil down to a simple question of stamina. If Sir Ivor lasted the mile and a half he would certainly win. If not, he wouldn't. Some of the breeding experts were convinced that he wouldn't get the trip, but I was convinced that he would stay ten furlongs, and in most Derbys that degree of stamina is enough, as the Epsom course does not make the sort of demands on the durability of a young horse that, say, The Curragh or Ascot do.

Sir Ivor was flown over from Ballydoyle on the Monday, two days before the race, and on the Tuesday I went down to work him on the track with his lead horse Belgrave, cantering him from the Derby start as far as the mile gate and then taking him steadily round Tattenham Corner in order to familiarise him with that famous bend. I had not set eyes on Sir Ivor since the Two Thousand Guineas and found him in wonderful condition: physically he was stronger and more filled out than at Newmarket, and mentally he seemed perfectly at one with himself, while even a steady descent of part of Tattenham Hill indicated that he had the necessary balance for a Derby horse.

As long as Sir Ivor stayed the distance, I knew I had little to fear from the twelve horses who opposed him. A couple of weeks after the Guineas I had ridden Petingo in the Prix Lupin at Longchamp. He failed to stay

Trainer Vincent O'Brien with Lester after Sir Ivor's Derby-eve workout, 28 May 1968.

Yellow Armlet

One Mile and a Half, for Three Yrs Old Entire
Colts and Fillies

3.35 The 189th Derby Stakes

£50,000 added to stakes
for three yrs old only, entire colts and fillies
ONE MILE AND A HALF
£30 to enter
£50 extra unless forfeit be declared by November 21st, 1967
£20 extra unless forfeit be declared by April 23rd, 1968
£50 extra unless forfeit be declared by May 14th, 1968
£50 extra if declared to run
The second 20%, third 10%, fourth 3% of the whole stakes
Weights: colts .... 9st; fillies 8st 9lb
THERE WILL BE A PARADE FOR THIS RACE
The Horserace Betting Levy Board have given £40,000 included in the value of this race
A Gold Trophy value £500 is also included in the value of this race
                                                                  A   SS
590 entries, 282 at £30, 203 at £80, 70 at £100, 21 at £150 and 14 at £200.—Closed February 22nd, 1967.

VALUES. WINNER £58,525 10s.; SECOND £17,330;
THIRD £8565; FOURTH £2429 10s.

Draw	Form			st	lb		
(10)	111	**301**	REMAND	9	0	LIGHT BLUE, PINK sash	
			Ch c Alcide—Admonish				
	J. Mercer		Mr J. J. Astor (W. Hern)				
(2)	202	**302**	MYRTUS	9	0	ROYAL BLUE, WHITE diamond and hooped sleeves, ORANGE cap	
			B c Mossborough—Picaresque				
	A. Murray		Mr N. Cohen (H. Price)				
(5)	311	**303**	LAUREATE	9	0	BLACK, WHITE cap	
			B c Aureole—Sundry				
	W. Carson		Lord Derby (B. van Cutsem)				
(4)	143	**304**	RIBERO	9	0	GREEN, YELLOW sleeves, SCARLET sash	
			B c Ribot—Libra				
	B. Taylor		Mr C. W. Engelhard (R. Johnson Houghton)				
(3)	111	**305**	SIR IVOR	9	0	CHOCOLATE, BLUE hoops and cap	
			B c Sir Gaylord—Attica				
	L. Piggott		Mr Raymond R. Guest (M. O'Brien, Ireland)				
(11)	212	**306**	TORPID	9	0	CRIMSON, SILVER braid	
			B c Match III—Cutter				
	G. Starkey		Mr R. D. Hollingsworth (J. Oxley)				
(12)	002	**307**	CONNAUGHT	9	0	BLACK, SCARLET cap	
			B c St Paddy—Nagaika				
	A. Barclay		Mr H. J. Joel (N. Murless)				
(9)	104	**308**	BENROY	9	0	BLACK, RED and YELLOW cross-belts and quartered cap	
			Br c Rockefella—Banka				
	D. Keith		Mr A. J. A. Kennedy (W. Nightingall)				

(Continued next page)

189th DERBY STAKES—continued

Draw	Form			st	lb		
(8)	043	**309**	FLORIANA	9	0	FRENCH GREY, SCARLET cuffs, cap and diamond hoop	
			B or br c Darius—Day Dawn				
	W. Rickaby		Mrs D. Langton (G. Hunter)				
(13)	314	**310**	SOCIETY	9	0	CERISE, GREY sleeves, GREY cap with CERISE hoops	
			Ch c Sheshoon—Blue Society				
	W. Williamson		Mr F. McMahon (P. Prendergast, Ireland)				
(6)	001	**311**	ATOPOLIS	9	0	BOTTLE GREEN, LIME GREEN and WHITE check cap	
			B c Acropolis—Tudor Top				
	A. Breasley		Mr R. N. Richmond-Watson (A. Budgett)				
(1)	000	**312**	FIRST RATE PIRATE	9	0	ROYAL BLUE and WHITE hoops, RED sleeves, BLUE cap	
			B c Barbary Pirate—Zarin Taj				
	P. Cook		Mr Billy Fury (R. Sturdy)				
(7)	0	**313**	ROYAL ROCKET	9	0	LIGHT BLUE, GREEN sash and striped sleeves	
			Gr c Sovereign Path—Farandole II				
	F. Durr		Mr R. J. Sigtia (G. Todd)				
(14)	011	**314**	MOUNT ATHOS	9	0	GREY, PINK sleeves, check cap	
			B c Sunny Way—Rosie Wings				
	R. Hutchinson		Mr A. J. Struthers (J. Dunlop)				

NUMBER OF DECLARED RUNNERS 14

The photograph used for the front cover of this racecard depicts the finish of the Derby 1967 with Royal Palace winning from Ribocco and has been reproduced by kind permission of Wiggins Teape Limited.

THREE-FIGURE NUMBERS ARE FOR ENTERING THE JACKPOT ONLY

The numbers in bold type will appear on saddle cloths and number boards and should be used for all other totalisator bets.

---

the ten and a half furlongs that day, and predictably it was announced that he would miss the Derby; he went on to become a top-class miler, winning the St James's Palace Stakes at Royal Ascot and the Sussex Stakes at Goodwood. The only runner other than Sir Ivor to start at single-figure odds in the 1968 Derby was Remand, who had been unbeaten as a two-year-old (I rode him when he won the Solario Stakes at Sandown Park and Royal Lodge Stakes at Ascot) and a few weeks before Epsom had won the Chester Vase. Second in that race had been Jim Joel's colt Connaught, a son of St Paddy whom Sir Ivor had beaten out of sight in the Guineas and who went into the Derby with not a single victory to his name. So Sir Ivor easily had the measure of those two, and his starting price of 4–5 was fully justified by the form book.

In those days the Derby field walked up from the parade ring – then situated way beyond the winning post – past the stands, then turned and cantered back past the winning post to the end of the course, from which point they would walk across the Downs to the Derby start along

Racecard for the 189th running of the Derby Stakes.

a path which before the big race was invariably teeming with enthusi-astic racegoers. These long-drawn-out preliminaries lasted at least twenty minutes and could place a great strain on a young horse, who had never seen such crowds before: the most placid three-year-old could easily become stirred up. Sir Ivor had not given any indication that he would have difficulty coping with all the pre-race activities, but Vincent as always left nothing to chance, sending his head lad Maurice O'Callaghan to meet the colt after the parade and walk him across the Downs to the start: Vincent's travelling head lad Gerry Gallagher led Sir Ivor up in the parade himself, but would then have to stay near the winning post to be reunited with the horse after the race.

Sir Ivor behaved impeccably. He didn't turn a hair in the paddock, during the parade ring or on the walk across the Downs, remained perfectly calm as we walked round before the start, and although there had been some slight worry about his possibly playing up at the stalls – his experience at Ascot might have left a mark – he went in without fuss and remained perfectly calm while the rest of the runners were loaded for what was only the second Derby to be started from stalls.

Opposite page:
In the parade.

Tattenham Corner, 1968:
Connaught leads into the
straight. Lester on Sir
Ivor is in the hooped
sleeves and light cap.

DAILY EXPRESS

I jumped him out, and on the uphill first couple of furlongs kept him handy towards the back of the pack while 150–1 outsider Benroy and Duncan Keith took the field along from Sandy Barclay on Connaught. Coming down the hill Benroy fell back beaten and Sandy sent Connaught into the lead – exactly the right tactic to make the most of Connaught's stamina and exploit any doubt about Sir Ivor's. I bided my time for most of the downhill stretch then gradually improved our position, and at Tattenham Corner we were in about seventh place, just behind Remand, as Connaught led into the straight. Once we straightened up Sandy really set Connaught alight and they went five lengths clear. Two furlongs out Remand, who had been trying to mount a challenge, started to weaken, while Mount Athos was straining to narrow the gap with the leader and I asked Sir Ivor to get closer. With a furlong to go it must have seemed that Connaught, still four lengths clear, could not be caught. But I knew Sir Ivor had the acceleration to catch the leader whenever I wanted, and however it may have looked from the stands, I did not feel any concern. When just inside the final furlong I thought the time had come and pulled Sir Ivor to the outside he hung fire for a moment, then seemed to understand what I was asking him to do and produced exactly the response I'd expected: he simply took off and flew past Connaught a hundred yards out, going past him so smoothly that I was able to ease him up for the last few strides. We won by a length and a half, with Mount Athos a further two and a half lengths back in third and Remand fourth, but the official distance was no true indication of Sir Ivor's superiority. That day he was simply in a different class from his rivals, and even I found his turn of foot astounding. Indeed, of all my nine Derby victories, 1968 on Sir Ivor was without question the most exciting.

Sadly Raymond Guest, winning his second Derby in the space of six years, could not be at Epsom to see Sir Ivor as his official duties kept him in Ireland, where he was required to be at the opening of the John F. Kennedy Memorial Park in County Wexford. So Sir Ivor was led into the winner's enclosure by his wife Carolyne Guest. But Mr Guest, who luckily had been able to watch the race on television in Ireland, was able to join us in London that evening for a celebration party at

Sir Ivor is led in by Carolyne Guest, wife of owner Raymond Guest. Vincent O'Brien is just behind the winner.

the Savoy Hotel, where a large television screen was erected at one end of the room so that we could replay the race over and over and I could explain to Sir Ivor's owner just how the Derby had been won. I was so absorbed in this that I paid no attention to another great sporting event taking place that day: Manchester United's extra-time victory over Benfica at Wembley to win the European Cup.

*   *   *

Sir Ivor, only the third American-bred horse to win the Derby after Iroquois (1881) and Lester's first winner Never Say Die, was the first odds-on Derby favourite since Tudor Minstrel, beaten into fourth in 1947 at odds of 4–7, and the first successful odds-on favourite in a running of the race at Epsom since Cicero, who won at 4–11 in 1905. (Gainsborough won at 8–13 in 1918, when the Derby was transferred to Newmarket during the First World War.) The 100–1 bet which Raymond Guest had struck with William Hill had proved some wager.

The press and Piggott's fellow jockeys, past as well as present, were united in their rapture at what was acclaimed as one of the great Derby victories –

and one of the great Derby rides. 'WHOOSH! IT'S SIR IVOR', read one headline; 'IT'S SIR IVOR THE GREAT', read another. 'Confidence and class characterised the whole performance', drooled the *Daily Mail*, while Bob Butchers in the *Daily Mirror* called it 'one of the greatest performances of race riding that Lester Piggott, or any other jockey for that matter, has ever executed. The sheer cheek of the champion had to be seen to be believed.' The *Daily Telegraph* waxed lyrical about 'a performance which for sheer style and flawless elegance has surely never been bettered on Epsom Downs.' In the *Daily Express* Clive Graham opened his report with the words: 'What a superb Derby this was. And what a triumph for supreme dedication and professionalism in all its aspects!' John Lawrence – now Lord Oaksey – wrote in the *Daily Telegraph*: 'I honestly believe that Mr Raymond Guest's Sir Ivor must be about as close as man has ever come to success in his long search for the ideal Thoroughbred', going on to call the Derby winner 'a beautiful, well-oiled machine who handles like a London taxi and accelerates like an Aston Martin. He is, in a word, perfection, and has in Vincent O'Brien and Lester Piggott the sort of accomplices that such perfection deserves.'

Sandy Barclay, who for at least a few seconds believed he had won the Derby at the age of nineteen, described the winner as 'the most brilliant horse I have ever seen', noting that 'Sir Ivor went past me as though he had just jumped in.' Ron Hutchinson, rider of Mount Athos, declared Sir Ivor 'a super horse – the best I've seen', and Jimmy Lindley, who rode the unplaced Atopolis, said that 'Lester has never ridden a greater or better judged race.' Lester's old rival Gordon Richards, by then a trainer, invoked the memory of a great trainer from an earlier generation when summing up the race: 'A great horse and a great jockey. As Fred Darling would have said – class.' Vincent O'Brien said of his charge: 'He is a prince of a horse and should have been named Prince Ivor and not Sir Ivor.' Dave Dick, one of few jockeys to have ridden big-race winners both on the Flat and over jumps, predicted: 'If you live to be a hundred you will never see such an exhibition of jockeyship.'

Even Lester's dentist Alastair MacDonald joined in the accolades, sending him a telegram which read: 'HEARTIEST CONGRATULATIONS STOP THANK HEAVEN YOUR RIDING IS OF A HIGHER QUALITY THAN YOUR TEETH.'

* * *

Extraordinary as it may sound after such an astonishing performance in the Derby, Sir Ivor proceeded to lose his next four races.

My agreement with Vincent O'Brien stipulated that his retained jockey Liam Ward would keep rides for the stable in Ireland, so for the Irish Derby at The Curragh I had to find an alternative. This turned out to be Ribero, who in his previous race at Ascot had been beaten twelve lengths by Connaught and seemed to have little hope of beating Sir Ivor. But I knew that for all the brilliance of his Derby victory Sir Ivor was much less likely to stay the mile and a half on a galloping track like The Curragh: obviously the level of stamina required to last out the trip on one course can be very different from that required at another, and the Derby course at Epsom, which is mostly downhill, can be got by a horse whose best trip is ten furlongs. So I rode Ribero to exploit that possible weakness in the 1–3 favourite. We took the lead as soon as we were round the final bend, and although Sir Ivor came to challenge us about two furlongs out, he seemed to die in Liam's hands and couldn't keep up the challenge. Ribero won by two lengths, and I have to say that I was not nearly as surprised by the overturning of Sir Ivor as most of the press seemed to be – not least because Ribero was, on his day, a top-class horse: later that year I won the St Leger on him after a dogged struggle with Bill Williamson on Canterbury, beating Connaught out of sight.

I was back on Sir Ivor for the Eclipse Stakes at Sandown Park, where we faced two absolutely top-notch horses in Royal Palace, who the previous year had won the Two Thousand Guineas and Derby, and the French four-year-old Taj Dewan, who earlier in 1968 had won the Prix Ganay at Longchamp. Sir Ivor started odds-on favourite, but seemed unwilling to let himself go when the race came to the crunch: perhaps he had been jarred up on the firm ground at The Curragh. Royal Palace and Taj Dewan had a furious battle in the final furlong and Sir Ivor tried valiantly to get to them, but all to no avail: Royal Palace beat the French horse by a short head, with Sir Ivor three quarters of a length back in third.

After that race Sir Ivor was very sore, and Vincent went fairly easy on him during his build-up to the Prix de l'Arc de Triomphe, to the extent that he was not fully wound up when just a week before the big

Raymond Guest, Lester and Sir Ivor after the colt's famous – and famously controversial – victory in the Washington DC International at Laurel Park, Maryland, 11 November 1968.

day at Longchamp he was beaten by Prince Sao in the Prix Henry Delamarre. In the Arc itself he ran a wonderful race but came up against one of the very best middle-distance horses of the post-war period in Vaguely Noble. Again pushing the limits of his stamina, Sir Ivor fought really hard and quickened under pressure, but Vaguely Noble always had his measure and won by three lengths.

Sir Ivor picked up the winning thread when cruising to victory in the Champion Stakes at Newmarket – Taj Dewan was well behind – then crossed the Atlantic to run in the Washington DC International at Laurel Park, Maryland. In those days there was nothing like the traffic of European horses across the Atlantic – indeed, Sir Ivor was the first Derby winner to run in the USA since Papyrus way back in 1923 – but the Washington International was an exceptionally valuable prize, and Raymond Guest was very keen to run his star horse in his native country. This turned out to be a very controversial race, and too much has been written about it already. Suffice it to say that in keeping Sir Ivor covered up behind horses on the inside until very late on, then producing him close home to unleash his great burst of acceleration and win easing down by three quarters of a length, I knew exactly what I was doing. The American press begged to differ, accusing me of nearly getting the best horse in the race beaten. One journalist wrote that 'If he were an American jockey he'd be crucified', but I knew more about Sir Ivor than the press did.

Sir Ivor did not run again, retiring first to the Ballygoran Stud in Ireland and then standing at the Claiborne Farm in Kentucky. Vincent O'Brien told me that Sir Ivor was the most intelligent horse he ever handled, and I have to admit to a particular affection for him. Years after his retirement I went to see him in his paddock at Claiborne, and he greeted me as if he knew exactly who I was!

When Sir Ivor was at stud in Ireland, Raymond Guest offered me the opportunity to send a mare of my own to the horse, and in 1969 I sent Limuru, who had not yet started to breed, to be covered by him. The result of this mating was Cavo Doro, on whom I finished second to Morston in the 1973 Derby.

For years people have asked me which was the best Derby winner I rode. All nine were great horses on the day, but Sir Ivor was the greatest. He had a superb conformation and his trademark was that incredible turn of foot, but his greatest quality was his sheer professionalism. More than any horse I ever rode, in the Derby or elsewhere, Sir Ivor knew what he was supposed to do, and always did his best to do it.

In short, Sir Ivor knew how to race.

* * *

Sir Ivor stayed on the stallion roster at Claiborne – where his offspring included Bates Motel and several top-class fillies including the 1976 Prix de l'Arc de Triomphe winner Ivanjica – until in 1991 at the age of twenty-six he was retired from stud duties. He remained in venerable retirement at Claiborne until on 10 November 1995 he was put down, at the age of thirty. At the time of his death he was the oldest Derby winner.

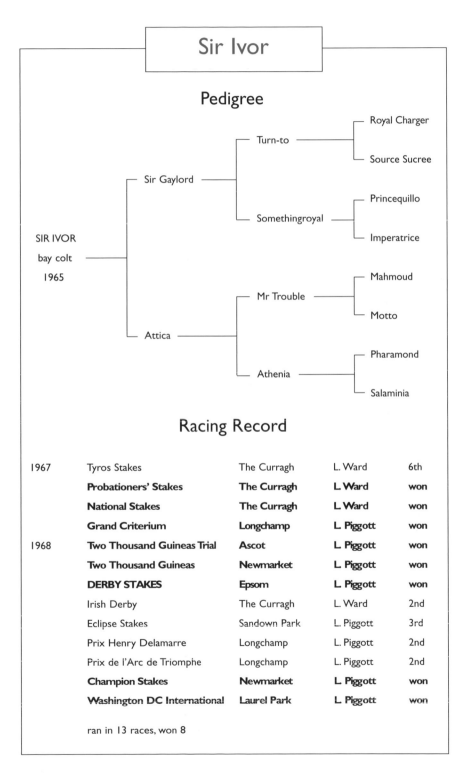

Sir Ivor

Pedigree

SIR IVOR
bay colt
1965

- Sir Gaylord
  - Turn-to
    - Royal Charger
    - Source Sucree
  - Somethingroyal
    - Princequillo
    - Imperatrice
- Attica
  - Mr Trouble
    - Mahmoud
    - Motto
  - Athenia
    - Pharamond
    - Salaminia

Racing Record

1967	Tyros Stakes	The Curragh	L. Ward	6th
	Probationers' Stakes	**The Curragh**	**L. Ward**	**won**
	National Stakes	**The Curragh**	**L. Ward**	**won**
	Grand Criterium	**Longchamp**	**L. Piggott**	**won**
1968	**Two Thousand Guineas Trial**	**Ascot**	**L. Piggott**	**won**
	Two Thousand Guineas	**Newmarket**	**L. Piggott**	**won**
	DERBY STAKES	**Epsom**	**L. Piggott**	**won**
	Irish Derby	The Curragh	L. Ward	2nd
	Eclipse Stakes	Sandown Park	L. Piggott	3rd
	Prix Henry Delamarre	Longchamp	L. Piggott	2nd
	Prix de l'Arc de Triomphe	Longchamp	L. Piggott	2nd
	Champion Stakes	**Newmarket**	**L. Piggott**	**won**
	Washington DC International	**Laurel Park**	**L. Piggott**	**won**

ran in 13 races, won 8

Opposite page:
*Venerable old age:
thirty-year-old Sir Ivor
at Claiborne Farm in
Kentucky, a few months
before his death in
November 1995.*

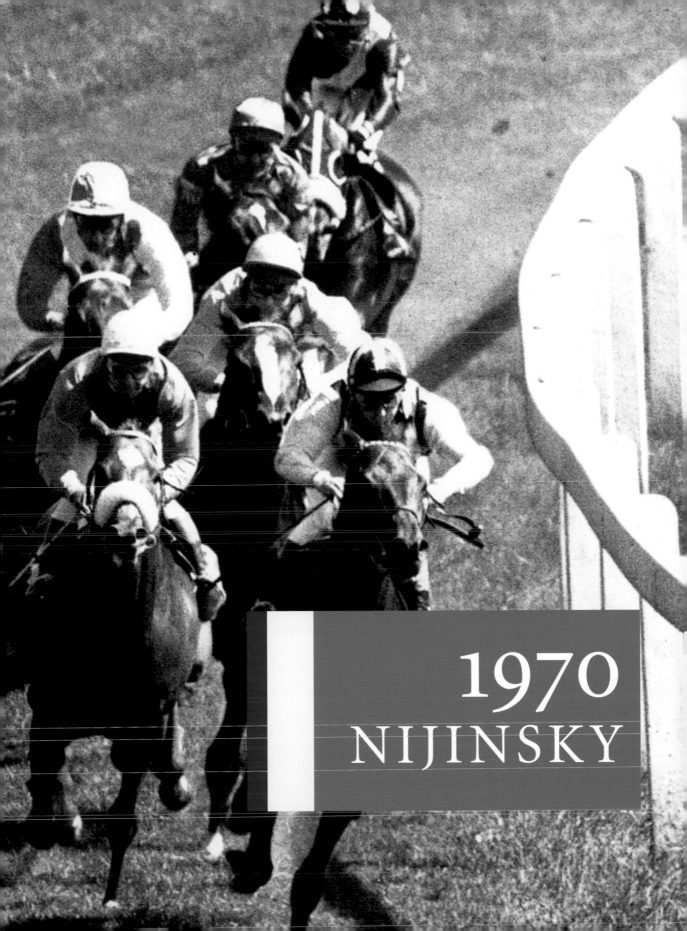

1970

NIJINSKY

Previous pages: *Tattenham Corner, 1970: Long Till (Duncan Keith) leads on the rails, with Meadowville (Geoff Lewis, centre) and Mon Plaisir (Jimmy Lindley) on his outside and Lester and Nijinsky just behind them. Gyr (Bill Williamson) is the white-faced horse towards the outside, being tracked by Stintino (Gerard Thiboeuf, hoops).*

191st Derby Stakes

3 June 1970
going: good
£62,311 to winner

1	**NIJINSKY**	**L. Piggott**	**11–8 fav**
2	GYR	W. Williamson	100–30
3	STINTINO	G. Thiboeuf	7–1
4	GREAT WALL	J. Mercer	80–1
5	Meadowville	G. Lewis	22–1
6	The Swell	R. Hutchinson	50–1
7	Approval	G. Starkey	13–2
8	Long Till	D. Keith	80–1
9	Cry Baby	A. Barclay	40–1
10	Tambourine Man	A. Murray	200–1
11	Mon Plaisir	J. Lindley	33–1

11 ran
distances: 2½ lengths, 3 lengths
time: 2 minutes 34.68 seconds
Winner bred by E. P. Taylor, owned by Charles W. Engelhard, trained at Ballydoyle, County Tipperary, by Vincent O'Brien

Although Lester himself may consider Sir Ivor the best Derby horse he ever rode, a poll of the racegoing public – who admittedly are in a less authoritative position to pronounce on the matter – would probably award that accolade to his next winner. Nijinsky remains one of the icons of racing history. Everything about him was special – his physique, his bearing, even his name, so resonant of class, grace and power. He exuded, as few racehorses have before or since, sheer charisma.

Charles W. Engelhard, the American owner of Nijinsky, had made his fortune in the minerals and chemicals business – and in particular in platinum – in the USA and South Africa. He had his first racehorses in Europe in the late 1950s – his first winner in Britain was Ticklish, trained by Peter Walwyn and ridden by Lester, in a Sandown Park handicap – and his first top-class horse was Romulus, one of the seven fallers in the 1962 Derby but winner that year of the Greenham Stakes, Sussex Stakes, Queen Elizabeth II Stakes and Prix du Moulin. Two years later Engelhard's colours – green, scarlet sash, yellow sleeves, green cap – were first carried to victory in a Classic when Indiana, runner-up to Santa Claus in the Derby, took the 1964 St Leger, while Lester's successes on Ribocco and Ribero, who landed the Irish Derby–St Leger double in 1967 and 1968 respectively, have been mentioned earlier. Engelhard had first attended the Derby in 1948, when witnessing the victory of My Love engendered in him a deep desire one day to own the winner of what he was to call 'the No. 1 race in the world'.

Vincent O'Brien's first Derby runner for Charles Engelhard had been Right Noble in 1966, and in 1968 Engelhard had heard very positive opinions of a Ribot yearling being prepared for the sales by the breeder E. P. Taylor at Windfields Farm, near Toronto. He asked O'Brien to go over and look at the horse. O'Brien did so, but was not pleased by what he saw: the colt had a crooked foreleg, and could not be recommended to Engelhard as a likely purchase. But Ballydoyle to Toronto was a long trip to look at just one horse, so O'Brien took time to study some of the other yearlings at the stud, and his eye was caught by a son of Northern Dancer, second living foal of the mare Flaming Page – a bright bay colt with three white feet and a heart-shaped star on his forehead.

Northern Dancer was the greatest horse in the history of Canadian racing. He won fourteen of his eighteen races, including the 1964 Kentucky Derby and Preakness (and would probably have won the US Triple Crown by winning the Belmont Stakes had his stamina not run out). He took up stud duties in 1965, his first foals being born the following year. Thus the colt out of Flaming Page – who could also boast a fine racing record, having won Canada's most prestigious race, the Queen's Plate (which Northern Dancer had himself won in 1964) – was from Northern Dancer's second crop in 1967. By the time that colt entered the sale ring in Canada in August 1968, few of Northern Dancer's first crop had yet begun to race, so as a sire he was an unknown quantity.

Even as a yearling Nijinsky had a real presence, and O'Brien was not alone in being attracted by him. Bidding was lively, and the price climbed until Engelhard's agent in the sale ring bid 84,000 Canadian dollars – a record for a bloodstock sale in that country – at which point the underbidder decided that enough was enough, and Engelhard had his colt, whom he named Nijinsky after the fabled ballet dancer Vaslav Nijinsky, who shortly before his death in 1950 had declared that he would be reincarnated as a horse.

Nijinsky arrived at Ballydoyle in September 1968, and immediately posed a problem. The staple feed at O'Brien's yard was oats, and Nijinsky declined to eat them, spending his early days in Ireland eating nothing other than hay. O'Brien phoned the stud manager of Windfields Farm for advice, and discovered that Nijinsky had never eaten oats, his basic diet in his native land being horse nuts, made from a compound of various foodstuffs. O'Brien asked for a supply of these nuts to be flown over to Ballydoyle straight away – and on the very day that they arrived Nijinsky decided that he may as well give oats a try, and found them perfectly palatable.

One problem was thus overcome, but another soon appeared. Nijinsky began to show distinct signs of temperament: it would prove difficult to persuade him to leave his box in the morning, he would rear up, tended to mess about on the gallops and show reluctance to get on with his exercise, and generally did not endear himself to the Ballydoyle staff. Early in 1969 O'Brien sent Charles Engelhard a report on his horse: 'I am somewhat concerned about Nijinsky's temperament and that he is inclined to resent getting on with his work. My best boys are riding him and we can only hope he will go the right way.'

Later in the spring that hope began to look as if it might be fulfilled, as Nijinsky responded to careful, sympathetic handling and not being bustled about. He was beginning to focus on his work more, and his gallops suggested he could well be an exceptional horse as long as his temperament did not get the better of him. By July 1969 he was ready to race.

Meanwhile in England another Derby had been and gone. In the 1969 race Lester rode in the Engelhard colours on Ribofilio, another son of Ribot trained by Fulke Johnson Houghton. Ribofilio had won the Two Thousand Guineas Trial at Ascot before running so badly when tailed off in the Two Thousand Guineas itself that an official dope test was ordered. It proved negative, and he started 7–2 favourite for an open-looking race at Epsom. A furlong out he was still in with a chance and trying to get into contention, but could not quite get to terms with the leaders and finished fifth behind Blakeney, beaten just over three lengths.

Nijinsky's first public appearance came six weeks after that Derby in the Erne Stakes at The Curragh on 12 July 1969, when he was ridden by stable jockey Liam Ward. It was well known that the horse was highly thought of at Ballydoyle: he started favourite at 4–11 and won as easily as an odds-on favourite should, though the official winning margin was just half a length from Everyday. Already he was being talked of in Ireland as the new Sir Ivor, and that view was underlined when he won two more races at The Curragh by the end of August: the Railway Stakes and the Anglesey Stakes, in both races starting 4–9. (Among the horses he beat in the Railway Stakes was a colt called Northern Monarch – none other than the Ribot colt Vincent O'Brien had rejected on his visit to Canada. He had not been sold, so E. P. Taylor sent him into training at Ballydoyle.) Next came the Beresford Stakes in late September, and again Nijinsky won easily. Four out of four in Ireland – ridden in all by Liam Ward – and it was time to go further afield and take on the top English two-year-olds in the Dewhurst Stakes at Newmarket, the first race in which he would be ridden by Lester.

* * *

I don't usually get too emotional about individual horses, but with Nijinsky it really was love at first sight – so commanding was his presence. Early in his two-year-old season he was not expected to be the star of Vincent's juveniles, as there was a horse in the yard named Great Heron, of whom big things were expected: he turned out to be a pretty good racehorse, but not remotely in the same league as Nijinsky. In those early days Nijinsky was very tense and had constant problems with his digestive system, so Vincent was keen to get a few races into him as a juvenile to help him settle down.

I did not sit on Nijinsky until getting legged up in the Newmarket paddock before the Dewhurst. This was his fifth race, and although the opposition was not up to the usual Dewhurst standard he won very easily indeed, striding away in the final furlong to beat Recalled, a son of Crepello, by three lengths. This made him hot favourite for both the Two Thousand Guineas and Derby in 1970, and I knew that, barring accidents, I would be unlikely to be looking elsewhere for my Derby ride.

Nijinsky did well through the winter, and made his seasonal reappearance as a three-year-old in the Gladness Stakes at The Curragh, the race named after Vincent's great mare on whom I had won the Gold Cup at Ascot in 1958. The Gladness Stakes was open to older horses as well as to three-year-olds, and among Nijinsky's opponents was the four-year-old Deep Run, who later would become the most influential National Hunt stallion in racing history. Ridden by Liam Ward, Nijinsky won by four lengths from Deep Run.

He then travelled to Newmarket at the end of April for the Two Thousand Guineas, for which he started at 4–7. This was the first time I'd seen him since the Dewhurst on the same course the previous October, and I was hugely impressed by his appearance: he had grown into a magnificent looking horse, and dominated the other runners in the parade ring beforehand. On the way to the start he gave me a marvellous feel, and an even more marvellous one on the way back. Early on I kept him well covered up behind the leaders, then about a furlong and a half out asked him to pick up – and he produced a tremendous turn of foot to sweep past Yellow God and Roi Soleil (on both of whom I'd won earlier that season) and win by two and a half lengths from Yellow God.

Early the following week a letter arrived at our home from Vaslav Nijinsky's widow Romola, who had been at Newmarket for the race: 'I was tremendously impressed with your magnificent winning of the Two Thousand Guineas race this afternoon on the beautiful horse

Nijinsky, and I send you my congratulations. I ask of you now only one thing – please win the Derby for us!' (I later learned that she had £25 on Nijinsky every time he raced, and she would have been at Epsom to watch the horse run in the Derby but for a late change of plan that detained her in Vienna.)

Like Sir Ivor, Nijinsky did not run between the Two Thousand Guineas and Derby, enjoying a quiet and trouble-free preparation at Ballydoyle. I went over there a week before the race and worked him over a mile. He was clearly in very good shape – in fact in much better shape than I was. Ten days before the Derby I had ridden at Longchamp on the Sunday, then at Sandown Park on the Monday, then flew back to Paris on the Monday evening to ride a gallop on Breton (on whom I'd won the Prix de Fontainebleau earlier in the season) for trainer Mick Bartholomew. By Tuesday afternoon I was back at Sandown – where I won the Temple Stakes on the great sprinter Raffingora – and then clambered into yet another plane to fly to Ballydoyle to ride Nijinsky in his pre-Derby gallop the following day. It was nearly dark by the time we flew into Tipperary, and Vincent's lads lit a bonfire to guide us in to the landing strip. After the gallop I had a quick breakfast with Vincent, then flew to Brighton, where I rode a double, then on to Paris to ride on Thursday, Newbury on Friday and Newmarket on Saturday.

By now I was feeling pretty exhausted, and as I was being legged up for my fifth ride on the Saturday I started feeling dizzy. This passed rapidly and I was able to ride in the race, but the racecourse doctor put his foot down after that and I missed my ride in the last. The weather had been very hot, I'd been wasting to do a very light weight on one of my Newmarket rides, and the rushing around must have had some effect, but none the less I was amazed when I got home and weighed myself: I was down to 7.12, half a stone below my usual riding weight. The Sunday papers were full of scare stories about how I might miss the Derby, but I was well enough to ride in Paris that day, and a couple of days off before Derby Day put me right.

Nijinsky was flown over from Ballydoyle on the Friday, five days before the Derby – not to Epsom, but to Sandown Park racecourse, where Vincent had made an arrangement for him to be stabled away from the glare of publicity at Epsom itself. The unbeaten Nijinsky was already being called a wonder horse, and although security at Epsom was tight, Vincent as usual was taking no chances, and to have flown him over later would have risked getting this still volatile colt stirred up too close to the big race.

On the Saturday he was taken out for a quiet trot around Sandown, then for brisker exercise on Sunday (though the 'wrong' way round at Sandown, to replicate the left-handed bends of Epsom) and the same sort of exercise on Monday, after which he was boxed the short distance to the racecourse stables at Epsom. On the Tuesday morning he was taken through the usual Derby-eve routine of Vincent's runners: accompanied by another horse of Vincent's named Riboprince, Nijinsky cantered from the Derby start to the top of the hill, then walked down to Tattenham Corner and hacked up the straight.

All seemed well, but as his lad was rubbing him down after this airing on the course, Nijinsky started pawing the ground, a sign of distress. Then he got down in his box and began sweating profusely, a symptom of colic. Vincent's own vet Demi O'Byrne was immediately flown over from Ballydoyle, but there was little to be done, as medication to ease his discomfort was out of the question so close to the race the following day. The only thing to do was to wait and to hope for the best. When after a couple of hours Nijinsky tentatively accepted a snack of grass mixed with bicarbonate of soda and bran, Vincent – who never left the horse's box – knew that the worst was over, and by the early evening the crisis had passed. Nijinsky was completely recovered, and news of the scare had not leaked out.

* * *

With only eleven runners, the 1970 Derby was short on quantity, but it was certainly not short on quality, with one newspaper preview going so far as to name it 'The Derby of the Century'. (Racing had already made the front pages two days before the Derby with the death on 31 May of Arkle, greatest of all steeplechasers.)

Nijinsky had three main challengers, and all of them boasted serious claims to be the first horse to lower his colours.

Judy and the Colonel

WHAT IS GOING TO WIN THE BIG RACE, COLONEL?

ENGLAND WILL LOOK TO *APPROVAL*, WHO WILL BE GALLOPING ON WHEN SOME OF THE OTHERS HAVE STOPPED...

THIS YEAR'S DERBY IS A TRULY INTERNATIONAL OCCASION. FRANCE HAS TWO CANDIDATES, *STINTINO*, WHO HAS DONE EVERYTHING THAT HE HAS BEEN ASKED... AND *GYR*, SEA BIRD'S BRILLIANT SON, WHO MIGHT NOT BE AT HIS BEST COMING DOWN THE HILL

BUT I SHALL RELY ON *NIJINSKY* WHO, I FEEL, WILL WIN IF HE LASTS OUT THE TRIP... AND WHO BETTER TO NURSE HIM HOME THAN *LESTER PIGGOTT*

Gyr, a son of Sea Bird II and like his sire trained in France by Etienne Pollet, was unbeaten as a three-year-old, having won the Prix Daru at Longchamp in April, showing an extraordinary turn of foot to swoop very late and win by a nose, and the Prix Hocquart at the same track in early May. A measure of his promise was that Pollet had put off retirement for a year in order to guide the colt through his three-year-old season. But he was a tall, rangy horse with an awkward action, and it was far from certain that he would act effectively over the bends and inclines of Epsom, where his regular jockey Bill Williamson was riding in his tenth Derby..

Another French-trained challenger was Stintino, trained by Etienne Pollet's former assistant Francois Boutin. Stintino came to Epsom unbeaten, having won two races as a juvenile, then at three taking the Prix de Guiche and Prix Lupin, both at Longchamp: in the latter he produced a brilliant performance to demolish a top-class field, including the Poule d'Essai des Poulains winner Caro and Sassafras, of whom we will be hearing more.

The home team was led by Approval, trained by Henry Cecil – Noel Murless's son-in-law, then in only his second season with a training licence. Approval had won the Observer Gold Cup at Doncaster as a two-year-old, and in his prep race before Epsom had easily won the Dante Stakes at York.

The Colonel crisply sums up the Derby for Judy in the Sun's *cartoon strip, drawn by George Stokes, 3 June 1970.*

But however good the form of his three main rivals, Nijinsky was the centre of attention, both for newspaper previews of the race and in the less likely arena of the political hustings. Prime Minister Harold Wilson had called a general election for 18 June 1970, and by Derby week campaigning was in full swing. Foreign Secretary George Brown attempted to touch a popular nerve when declaring in one campaign speech in North Walsham in Norfolk two days before the Derby that he would be backing Nijinsky: 'The odds aren't good but I'd rather be on a winner than a loser – that's why I'm saying vote Labour as well.' (Labour lost.)

George Brown's observation that the odds about Nijinsky were not good would not wash with any punter familiar with the concept of 'value' in betting, as the colt's starting price of 11–8 was the only time in his entire career that he started at odds against. The rest of the market demonstrated that this was essentially a four-horse race: Gyr was second favourite at 100–30 with Approval 13–2 and Stintino 7–1; the next horse in the market was Lingfield Derby Trial winner Meadowville at 22–1.

* * *

As I saw it, there were only three reasons why Nijinsky wouldn't win the Derby.

Firstly, he had never raced over further than one mile, and it was conceivable that he might not possess the stamina for a trip half as long again. His sire Northern Dancer's stamina had been found wanting over a mile and a half in the Belmont Stakes, but he won several major races over ten furlongs, and Nijinsky's dam Flaming Page had, like Northern Dancer, won the Queen's Plate in Canada over that trip. More to the point, Nijinsky had such a relaxed manner of racing and was wonderfully malleable, so there was no chance of his burning himself out by running too freely early on.

Secondly, he might get stirred up during the preliminaries and waste too much nervous energy before he got to the serious business of the afternoon. Nijinsky's highly charged temperament seemed to have been inherited from his dam and was the cause of a niggling worry throughout his career. All we could do on Derby Day was keep him as calm as possible.

The third question was the one which applies to every Derby runner: would he act on the course? Nijinsky was a big horse (another inheritance from Flaming Page, who was a large mare while Northern Dancer was much more compact) and there was real concern that he might be all at sea around Epsom. On the other hand, he was wonderfully well balanced.

What did not bother me unduly was the strength of the opposition. Approval had shown good form and Stintino was unbeaten, but to me the only real danger was Gyr, and my tactic was simply to ride to beat him. Gyr was such a tall and ungainly horse, however, that I thought he would have a real problem handling the track.

The race before the Derby was the Woodcote Stakes for two-year-olds, in which I rode My Swallow, the odds-on favourite. My Swallow was owned by the television rental magnate David Robinson, and I had ridden the colt when he won his only previous race, the Zetland Stakes at York in May. He won the Woodcote Stakes comfortably enough, and I rode him again the following month when he beat Mill Reef a short head in the Prix Robert Papin at Maisons-Laffitte in France. At the end of the season My Swallow was officially rated the best two-year-old in Europe, one pound ahead of Mill Reef and two pounds ahead of Brigadier Gerard. I can't claim that I knew for sure at Epsom just how brilliant he would become, but it was a good start to Derby Day.

Nijinsky looked superb in the parade ring and went through the Derby preliminaries without getting agitated in any way, and the race itself proved the most straightforward Derby I ever rode in. With only eleven runners it was simple to keep Nijinsky in the position I wanted on the uphill stretch from the start as the outsiders Cry Baby and Long Till made the early pace. He was on the bridle and going easily all the way down the hill – which he handled beautifully – and at Tattenham Corner was about fifth, with Bill Williamson and Gyr on our outside. Stintino was towards the rear, and I knew that I only had Gyr to worry about, as Approval was already back-pedalling. Early in the straight Gyr made his move, getting to the front with a quarter of a mile to go and striding clear. Stintino started making headway, and for a moment it might have

Nijinsky powers home from Gyr, with Stintino third and Great Wall (Joe Mercer) fourth.

looked as if Nijinsky, racing between the two, was going to have a struggle on his hands. Then I showed him the whip, gave him a couple of cracks, and he instantly changed gear, leaving Stintino behind and surging past Gyr in a matter of strides. I was able to ease him up before the winning post, where he won by two and a half lengths from Gyr, with Stintino three lengths further behind and Great Wall fourth.

The occasion of my fifth Derby winner was the first on which I was invited up to the Royal Box, along with Charles Engelhard and Vincent, to be presented to the Queen. That evening there was a party at Annabel's, the famous night club in London, and one of my abiding memories of that day is of the crate of Coca-Cola beside Mr Engelhard's chair being steadily emptied by Nijinsky's owner, who had a consuming passion for the drink which bordered on addiction. Long before the dessert was served he had fallen sound asleep, oblivious to the raucous celebration raging around him.

* * *

While Engelhard snored on, the press was ratcheting up the superlatives for the following morning's editions. Peter Scott in the *Daily Telegraph* described Nijinsky's victory as 'a display of sheer brilliance', and in the same paper John Lawrence wrote: 'Perfection in any form is as hard to describe as it is delightful to watch, but there was no mistaking it at Epsom yesterday. As Lester Piggott and Nijinsky swept home together in the sunshine, the whole sport of racing glowed with a mixture of admiration, pride and pleasure.' For Clive Graham in the *Daily Express,* 'This was a great Derby, won by a horse-loving amateur as owner, two master craftsmen, trainer and jockey, and, above all, by a colt who has placed himself among the real champions.' Graham's colleague Peter O'Sullevan described how two and a half furlongs out it simply appeared to be a matter of by how far Gyr would win: 'But in these situations before counting gains you must always look for Piggott. And there he was, sitting, waiting, and finally launching the irrepressible power of the

Portrait of Lester and Nijinsky by Madeline Selfe.

Previous pages:
*Charles Engelhard
(extreme right) greets
his returning hero.*

Engelhard champion, to whom no horse has yet found a reply in eight races.' In the *Daily Mail*, Jim Stanford wrote: 'Nijinsky and Lester Piggott turned the final stages of the 191st running of the Derby yesterday into an exhibition of their unparalleled talents.' The *Sun* (still a broadsheet in those days) headlined Nijinsky as 'THE HORSE THAT COST THE BOOKIES £3 MILLION', though elsewhere Cyril Stein, chairman of Ladbroke's, was quoted as saying that 'our betting shops all seem to have won on the race. We expected to lose at least £100,000 if Nijinsky won. As it is we have lost only £50,000 – because the punters unaccountably deserted Lester.' On the Sunday following the Derby, Richard Baerlein in the *Observer* described Nijinsky as 'possibly the greatest Derby winner of them all'.

Such an assessment was supported by the time of the race, which at 2 minutes 34.68 seconds usurped Crepello's position as the fastest since Mahmoud's record 2 minutes 33.8 in 1936 (a clocking which Richard Baerlein considered could be taken 'with a pinch of salt') to become the second fastest in Derby history.

Charles Engelhard – whose nerves during the race had been so taut that he watched the face of his racing manager David McCall rather than the action itself – was winning the Derby for the first time after Indiana in 1964 and Ribocco in 1967 had run second. Vincent O'Brien was winning for the third time, and became the only trainer in history to have won three Derbys and three Grand Nationals. For Lester it was a fifth Derby and a sixteenth Classic.

* * *

The rest of the Nijinsky story has often been related.

Liam Ward still had an agreement to ride Vincent's horses in Ireland, so he was in the saddle when Nijinsky won the Irish Derby at the end of June. I took the ride on Meadowville, who had been well beaten when fifth in the Derby, and he ran well to finish second behind Nijinsky, who cruised in by three lengths.

I was reunited with Nijinsky in the King George VI and Queen Elizabeth Stakes at Ascot in late July. This was the first time he faced the cream of the older generation, and he was the only three-year-old in a field of six which included the 1969 Derby winner Blakeney; the 1968 Italian Derby winner Hogarth; Karabas, on whom I had won the 1969 Washington DC International; Caliban, who the day after Nijinsky's Derby had beaten the great mare Park Top and me in the Coronation Cup; and Crepellana, a daughter of Crepello who had won the Prix de Diane – French Oaks – in 1969. These were all high-class horses, but Nijinsky demolished them with a burst of acceleration a furlong out which if anything was more remarkable than his change of gear in the Derby. I eased him right down approaching the line, and the official margin of two lengths by which he beat Blakeney was a huge understatement of his superiority. He had been pitched in against the best older horses and yet still won in a canter, and for me that was his finest moment. That day he was the most impressive horse I ever sat on.

The St Leger in mid-September – and thus the Triple Crown – now looked even more of a formality for Nijinsky, but at that stage it was by no means certain that he would run in that race. His principal target was the Prix de l'Arc de Triomphe in Paris in early October, and Vincent's programme of training would be geared towards that race, victory in which would confirm Nijinsky's huge worth as a stallion as well as his towering status as a racehorse.

But the week after the King George he contracted American ringworm, a particularly nasty skin condition which caused most of his hair to fall out and greatly diluted his energy. Maintaining an orthodox training routine was out of the question, as Nijinsky was in no state to have a saddle put on him, let alone be galloped. He was led out of his box each day and occasionally lunged, and if he was to have any chance of getting to the Arc it seemed inevitable that he would have to miss the St Leger, which apart from all other considerations was two and half furlongs longer than he had ever raced before, and hardly the ideal preparation for the most important race of his life.

A complicating factor in an already difficult situation for Vincent was that Charles Engelhard's health was deteriorating. Well aware that a Triple Crown victory for Nijinsky would bring his owner Turf immortality, Mr Engelhard prevailed upon Vincent to get Nijinsky to Doncaster for the St Leger if he possibly could, and when the horse

showed distinct signs of recovery his training regime was restructured with the final Classic of the season as the first target.

Nijinsky duly appeared at Doncaster. I had not clapped eyes on him since Ascot, and to my mind the gleam in his eye was a little dimmed, and he seemed quieter than usual as we went through the preliminaries before the race. Of course, he was maturing, and each successive race helped calm him down, so I was not unduly alarmed by this more placid demeanour, but I did wonder whether he was still feeling the after-effects of his illness.

He duly won the race – by a length from Meadowville – and basked in the glory of being the first colt to win the Triple Crown since Bahram in 1935, and only the fifteenth in the history of racing in England. But I knew that behind the apparent ease of his victory he was no longer the horse he had been in the summer: despite appearances, he was all out at the end of the St Leger, and unlike at Epsom, The Curragh or Ascot could not have won by much more than he did.

Back at Ballydoyle, it transpired that Nijinsky had lost twenty-nine pounds of body weight through his Doncaster effort, a huge amount for a horse who had seemed to win so cosily. Although it was still the intention to run him in the Arc, to me he was no longer the certainty that I would have considered him before his illness.

Longchamp on Arc day is always packed, but in 1970 it was heaving with people who had come to see Nijinsky. Too many of these worshippers were inside the paddock, and with camera crews and photographers fighting in a desperate scrum to get shots of the most famous horse in the world on his biggest day, Nijinsky became very stirred up. By the time I walked into the parade ring with the other jockeys he was pouring sweat, and there was a look of panic in his eye.

We were drawn on the outside of the fifteen-runner field – which included Gyr and Stintino – and Nijinsky found it difficult to keep his place early on, a problem compounded by the fact that the rules in France forbade crossing to the inside rail until a furlong of the race had been covered. We tried to progress through the field, but with half a mile to go were still further back than I wanted to be, and then were blocked by several horses as I tried to improve Nijinsky's position on

Opposite page:
Nijinsky in his pomp, minutes before winning the St Leger – and thus the Triple Crown – at Doncaster, 12 September 1970.

the last bend, forcing us to the outside. The final straight at Longchamp is very short, and by the time we had got back on an even keel Sassafras, ridden by my old friend Yves Saint-Martin, was in front on the rails and going for home for all he was worth. Nijinsky did his level best to catch up and for a moment got his nose in front, but under the pressure of his effort he began to hang to the left, and close home simply could find no more. We were beaten a head.

I had scarcely pulled Nijinsky up before the shower of criticism started pelting down on my head – most of it accusing me of laying too far out of my ground. While the critics had not ridden in the race and I had, it was certainly the case that Nijinsky would have won the Arc if he had not been so comprehensively blocked in the closing stages, and if he had not veered left under pressure close home. But he had been beaten and that was that.

Defeat in the Arc – the first of Nijinsky's career – encouraged Vincent and Mr Engelhard to give the colt one more outing so that he could bow out on a winning note, and the only feasible opportunity was the Champion Stakes at Newmarket, just thirteen days after the race in Paris. But the less said about the Champion Stakes the better. The moment I saw Nijinsky in the parade ring I could tell that he had not got over the Arc experience: he was a nervous wreck, and the huge crowd which had turned out to bid him farewell just made matters worse. In the race he never gave me the old feeling, and when I asked him to go on and win there was precious little response. He was beaten one and a half lengths by Lorenzaccio, a good horse owned by my friend Charles St George but not remotely in the same league as Nijinsky in his prime. Clearly his illness before the St Leger had affected him mentally, and that in turn affected his racing performance.

Nijinsky did not run again after Newmarket, and sadly Charles Engelhard did not live long to bask in the glory of his greatest horse, as he died in March 1971, aged only fifty-four. I had ridden his first winner in England, had won five Classics and many other big races in his colours, and always found him a wonderfully enthusiastic and generous owner.

Nijinsky himself took up stud duties at Claiborne Farm in Kentucky, where I would visit him – and Sir Ivor, who was at the same stud – in later years whenever I was in the area. Even in his old age he still gave off that sense that he knew he was something very special, which indeed he was. Nijinsky had more sheer natural racing ability than any other horse I ever rode, and in the summer of 1970 he was indisputably one of the greatest racehorses of the century.

∗   ∗   ∗

The valuation put on Nijinsky when he was syndicated to stand at Claiborne was $5.44 million, which made him the most valuable stallion in the world, but before long that figure seemed far from unreasonable. For he was an outstanding success as a sire, his offspring including three Derby winners: Golden Fleece in 1982, Shahrastani in 1986, and Lammtarra (who also won the King George and Arc) in 1995. Two other Derby winners, Kahyasi (1988) and Generous (1991) were his grandsons. Other distinguished names in the Nijinsky progeny include Green Dancer, Ile de Bourbon, Niniski, Kings Lake, Caerleon, Quiet Fling, Gorytus, Solford, Shadeed, Ferdinand, Dancing Spree, Snow Bride and Royal Academy.

Such a record makes it even more galling for British breeders that negotiations to secure his breeding services for the National Stud should have foundered shortly before the 1970 Derby. Peter Burrell, former Director of the Stud, placed the blame for this squarely at the door of George Wigg, chairman of the Horserace Betting Levy Board. Burrell wrote in his autobiography how he had been planning the purchase of Nijinsky: 'All I needed was [Wigg's] approval, but when I met him at Epsom on the Tuesday and told him the position, I was ordered to have nothing more to do with it and to leave it to him. I don't know what he did but the deal fell through. The loss to the National Stud and British Thoroughbred breeding cannot be computed.' What appears to have happened is that Wigg had made arrangements with the Treasury to obtain dollars up to the equivalent of £2 million but had no intention of bidding the full amount for the services of the horse, and withdrew from negotiations when he learned that Tim Rogers, Chairman of the Irish Breeders' Association, had made a firm offer of £2 million. But this had not been enough. Engelhard had been building up his breeding interests in the USA and was keen to make the best horse he had ever owned or would ever own a cornerstone of that operation.

Nijinsky remained in active service at Claiborne until 1992, when worsening health caused him to be put down at the age of twenty-five.

Wherever the experts might rank him in the pantheon of great horses of the twentieth century, there was an undeniable magic about Nijinsky which transcends ratings or form lines. One small fact which underlines how everything about this extraordinary racehorse was of the highest class is that the video of his career, *A Horse Called Nijinsky*, was narrated by Orson Welles: one legend telling the story of another.

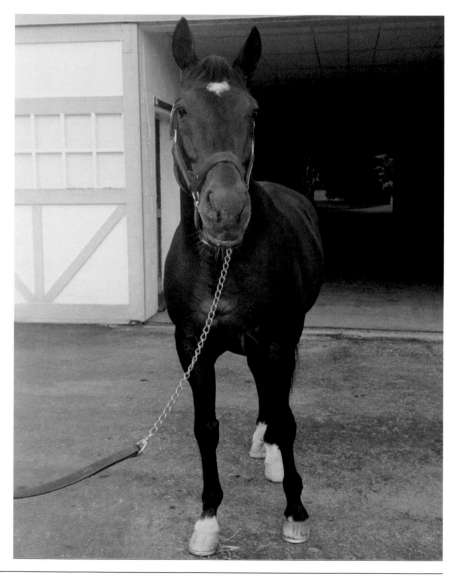

Nijinsky, aged twenty-two, at Claiborne Farm, Kentucky, September 1989.

Nijinsky

Pedigree

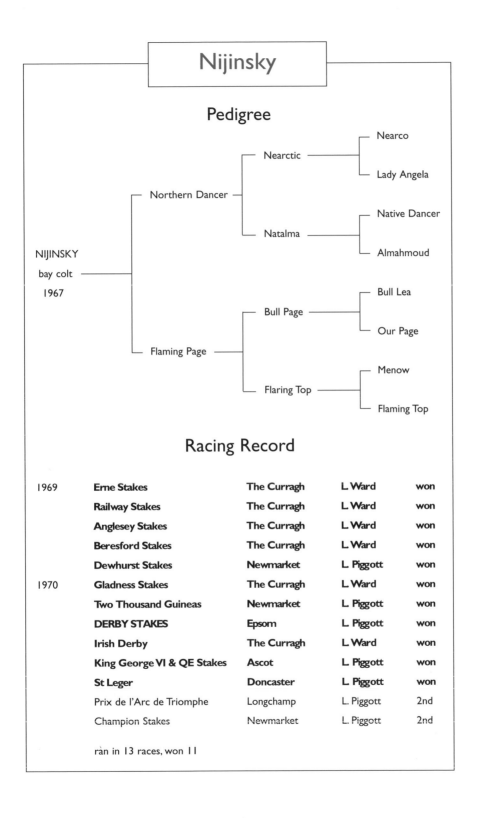

NIJINSKY
bay colt
1967

- Northern Dancer
  - Nearctic
    - Nearco
    - Lady Angela
  - Natalma
    - Native Dancer
    - Almahmoud
- Flaming Page
  - Bull Page
    - Bull Lea
    - Our Page
  - Flaring Top
    - Menow
    - Flaming Top

Racing Record

Year	Race	Course	Jockey	Result
1969	**Erne Stakes**	**The Curragh**	**L. Ward**	**won**
	Railway Stakes	**The Curragh**	**L. Ward**	**won**
	Anglesey Stakes	**The Curragh**	**L. Ward**	**won**
	Beresford Stakes	**The Curragh**	**L. Ward**	**won**
	Dewhurst Stakes	**Newmarket**	**L. Piggott**	**won**
1970	**Gladness Stakes**	**The Curragh**	**L. Ward**	**won**
	Two Thousand Guineas	**Newmarket**	**L. Piggott**	**won**
	DERBY STAKES	**Epsom**	**L. Piggott**	**won**
	Irish Derby	**The Curragh**	**L. Ward**	**won**
	King George VI & QE Stakes	**Ascot**	**L. Piggott**	**won**
	St Leger	**Doncaster**	**L. Piggott**	**won**
	Prix de l'Arc de Triomphe	Longchamp	L. Piggott	2nd
	Champion Stakes	Newmarket	L. Piggott	2nd

ran in 13 races, won 11

EPSOM

6

7 6

1972
ROBERTO

Previous pages:
*The official photofinish
print of the 1972 Derby:
Lester on Roberto beats
Rheingold (Ernie
Johnson) by a short
head.*

193rd Derby Stakes

7 June 1972
going: firm
£63,735.75 to winner

1	**ROBERTO**	**L. Piggott**	**3–1 fav**
2	RHEINGOLD	E. Johnson	22–1
3	PENTLAND FIRTH	Pat Eddery	50–1
4	OUR MIRAGE	F. Durr	100–1
5	Gombos	C. Roche	50–1
6	Scottish Rifle	R. Hutchinson	22–1
7	Ormindo	B. Taylor	20–1
8	Steel Pulse	W. Pyers	9–1
9	Moulton	E. Hide	45–1
10	Meadow Mint	W. Carson	50–1
11	Manitoulin	W. Swinburn	66–1
12	Charling	J. Lindley	28–1
13	Sukawa	Y. Saint-Martin	66–1
14	Palladium	J. Higgins	66–1
15	Lyphard	F. Head	4–1
16	Mercia Boy	R. Marshall	200–1
17	Yaroslav	G. Lewis	4–1
18	Paper Cap	J. Gorton	200–1
19	Donello	J. Mercer	200–1
20	Young Arthur	A. Murray	200–1
21	Mezzanine	P. Waldron	200–1
22	Neptunium	A. Barclay	35–1

22 ran
distances: short head, three lengths
time: 2 minutes 36.09 seconds
Winner bred and owned by John Galbreath,
trained at Ballydoyle, County Tipperary, by Vincent O'Brien

There was no Nijinsky on the horizon at the beginning of the 1971 season, but there was the next best thing: his full brother Minsky, who raced in the colours which Charles Engelhard's widow Jane had taken over on the death of her husband. Minsky won the Gladness Stakes and The Tetrarch Stakes at The Curragh but was no match for Brigadier Gerard, Mill Reef and My Swallow in the Two Thousand Guineas – he finished fourth behind that distinguished trio – and was not trained for the Derby.

This left Lester in the unusual position of still being without a ride as May wore on and the big day at Epsom got ever nearer. He had his offers, of course, and eventually revived his association with Noel Murless when agreeing to ride The Parson, who had shown some promise as a two-year-old despite finishing unplaced in both his races, and on his first outing at three had run second to Fair World in the Dante Stakes at York. By now Noel Murless's stable jockey was Geoff Lewis, but Lewis had a special arrangement which allowed him to ride the Ian Balding-trained Mill Reef in the Derby – hence the opportunity for Lester to ride once more for Warren Place. The Parson started at 16–1 at Epsom, and ran respectably to finish sixth behind Mill Reef, one of the greatest Derby winners only a year after another.

The outstanding two-year-old of 1971 was Crowned Prince, trained at Newmarket by Bernard van Cutsem and owned by Frank McMahon, co-owner with Bing Crosby of Meadow Court. A full brother to 1969 Kentucky Derby and Preakness winner Majestic Prince, Crowned Prince had cost $510,000 as a yearling at auction in Keeneland, Kentucky – by a long margin a record for that prestigious sale – and great things were expected of him. Ridden by Lester in his first race at Newmarket in August 1971, he started at 2–7 but could finish only sixth, then won his next two races, the Champagne Stakes at Doncaster and the Dewhurst Stakes at Newmarket (ridden in both by Lester) so impressively that he became winter favourite for the 1972 Two Thousand Guineas and Derby. (Runner-up in both the Champagne Stakes and Dewhurst was Rheingold, who features prominently in this story a little later on.)

Meanwhile over at Ballydoyle there was talk of a new superstar in the shape of Roberto, who even before he had set foot on a racecourse was, it was reliably reported, having Vincent O'Brien making favourable comparisons with Sir Ivor and Nijinsky. Roberto had been bred by his owner John Galbreath, a building tycoon based in Ohio, who as well as having several studs in Kentucky owned the Pittsburgh Pirates, a leading American baseball team. Roberto was named after the Pirates' star player Roberto Clemente.

Roberto won his first three races at The Curragh – his maiden by three lengths, the Anglesey Stakes by six and the National Stakes by five. In all these Roberto had been ridden by Vincent O'Brien's new stable jockey Johnny Roe, but Lester partnered the colt in his first race outside Ireland, the Grand Criterium at Longchamp in October 1971: here Roberto was beaten for the first time, finishing fourth behind Hard To Beat but running well enough to keep Classic hopes alive.

By the spring of 1972 Lester had a tough choice between Crowned Prince and Roberto for the Two Thousand Guineas – and, if his horse came well enough through that race, the Derby. He decided to go with Crowned Prince and committed himself to riding that colt in the Two Thousand Guineas, at which point Vincent O'Brien booked the Australian jockey Bill Williamson for Roberto.

Bill Williamson had moved to Ireland in 1960 from his native Australia, where his biggest win had been the 1952 Melbourne Cup on Dalray. In 1962 he moved to England, where by 1972 his many big-race victories included the One Thousand Guineas twice and the Ascot Gold Cup. He rode consecutive winners of the Prix de l'Arc de Triomphe on Vaguely Noble in 1968 (with Lester runner-up on Sir Ivor) and Levmoss in 1969. By the spring of 1972 he was forty-nine years old and coming towards the end of his career – he had ridden his first winner in 1937 – but was still one of the most sought-after jockeys in Europe.

* * *

When I saw Crowned Prince in the parade ring before his first race of that season, the Craven Stakes at Newmarket, I had no reason to question whether I'd made the right choice. He looked superb, and had clearly wintered very well. The race should have been a formality for him and he started at 4–9, but when a quarter of a mile out I asked him to pick up he showed no response whatsoever, and finished fourth behind a colt of Noel Murless's named Leicester. The general reaction to this defeat was one of shock, and he was immediately removed from the Two Thousand Guineas betting, but I still thought that he could be a Guineas horse: the Craven Stakes was his first run of the season and the ground was on the soft side for him, so there was every chance that he would improve significantly by the time of the Classic two and a half weeks later. Ten days after the Craven Stakes, Bernard van Cutsem took him for a gallop at Yarmouth racecourse, after which he announced that the colt had a respiratory problem and would never race again. He was retired to stud in Ireland.

By then it was much too late to get back on Roberto for the Two Thousand Guineas, so I accepted the ride on Grey Mirage (who later became the sire of Desert Orchid) for Bill Marshall, a trainer for whom I'd often ridden in the past. We finished well behind the winner High Top — Willie Carson's first Classic winner — who beat Roberto half a length. High Top was trained, like Crowned Prince, by Bernard van Cutsem, and at home was not considered as good as his now sidelined stable companion.

Like Nijinsky and Sir Ivor (and indeed Never Say Die), Roberto was American-bred, a son of Hail To Reason, who had been champion two-year-old in the USA in 1960, out of the mare Bramalea, who won eight races including the Coaching Club American Oaks. This was a high-class pedigree and there was not much doubt that Roberto would stay the mile and a half of the Derby, but he was Bill Williamson's ride in the big race, and as far as I was concerned that was that: I had to find myself another horse.

The racing papers must have been short of something important to write about in the weeks after the Guineas, as my Derby ride became a subject of intense speculation, little of it based on much knowledge of the facts. My name was first linked with Boucher, a son of Ribot trained at Ballydoyle, who was removed from the Derby reckoning after finishing last in the Chester Vase. (He was diagnosed as having a particularly nasty virus, but recovered later in the season and I won the St Leger on him.) Speculation next connected me with the French-trained Hard To Beat, who was then re-routed to the Prix du Jockey-Club at Chantilly, where he gave me my one and only victory in the French equivalent of the Derby; with Gombos, trained in Ireland by Paddy Prendergast; with Pentland Firth, winner of the Classic Trial at Sandown

Park and then runner-up in the Predominate Stakes at Goodwood; and with Martinmas, who had won the Greenham Stakes at Newbury, as had his stable companion Mill Reef the year before en route to his Derby victory. I finally settled on Manitoulin, who had won the Royal Whip at The Curragh in the middle of May: he was trained by Vincent and owned by the wife of Roberto's owner John Galbreath.

On Saturday 27 May, eleven days before the Derby, Bill Williamson took a crashing fall off a horse named The Broker in a race at Kempton Park. At first it looked as if his shoulder was so badly damaged that he might be ruled out of the Derby ride on Roberto, but within a couple of days he seemed to be recovering well and looked likely to make Epsom without difficulty.

After racing at Sandown Park on the Tuesday, eight days before the race, Susan and I flew across to Ballydoyle, and the following morning I worked Manitoulin. I cannot claim that the experience gave me much optimism: Manitoulin was not nearly as good as Roberto, and even though he might run into a place, his prospects of winning the Derby looked pretty slim.

But then events took a different turn. By the weekend before the Derby Bill Williamson – popularly known as 'Weary Willie' on account of his usual expression – was not recovering from his fall as quickly as had been expected, and Mr Galbreath was becoming very concerned. Bill had gone to London to see Bill Tucker, the renowned orthopaedic physician, and Tucker reported to Vincent that the only way of knowing whether the shoulder was healed would be to see what happened when Bill rode a horse again. But John Galbreath was convinced that Bill could not be fit enough to ride in the Derby – which for any jockey is a more than usually demanding race – and on the Monday afternoon, with forty-eight hours to go before the race, asked Vincent to put me on standby. When Vincent called to tell me this I did not raise any objection.

That Monday evening Mr Galbreath, who had flown in from Kentucky only the previous day, invited Vincent and Bill up to his suite at Claridge's, where he broke the news to Bill that I would be riding Roberto, not him, and a statement to the press to that effect was issued. Mr Galbreath softened the blow with the undertaking that if the horse won, Bill would receive the same percentage of the prize money as I would get.

On the Tuesday morning all hell broke loose in the newspapers – 'DERBY STORM OVER PIGGOTT', 'PIGGOTT SPARKS BIG RACE ROW', and so on – but by the time Bill reached Salisbury that afternoon for his first ride since the fall I had already taken Roberto out for a quiet piece of exercise at Epsom and was very pleased with the feel he gave me. Bill came through that Salisbury ride – his only one of the afternoon – in one piece, but that didn't necessarily mean that he was fit enough to ride in a race like the Derby: at least, that's what Mr Galbreath thought, and there was no question of his changing his mind.

The press tore into me for 'jocking off' a fellow rider – and, to a lesser extent, into Mr Galbreath and Vincent – but for me the decision was perfectly reasonable. Roberto was Mr Galbreath's horse, and he could say who rode him, and in any case, if Bill had been properly fit, why was he unable to ride in a race until the day before the Derby? Mr Galbreath's gesture of offering him the same cut of the prize money as

As the storm rages in the press, Lester and Roberto have a quiet moment at Epsom on the day before the Derby. In front of them is Manitoulin, ridden by Johnny Brabston.

myself was generous, but the owner could surely be allowed to be uncompromising in wanting to get his horse the best ride possible for the most important race of his life, and as far as I was – and am – concerned there's no more to it.

* * *

Justified or not, the replacing of Bill Williamson was the most controversial episode in Lester's whole Derby history, though some observers were less surprised by the very late turn of events than others. Reporting from Chantilly on the Sunday before the Derby, Peter O'Sullevan had written in Monday's *Daily Express* that 'a significant item to emerge on this sultry afternoon ... was that a further change of Epsom Derby partner for Lester Piggott is not now inconceivable.' Those numerate enough to put two and two together went straight round the betting shop to get on Roberto before the news was officially broken on Tuesday, the day before the race, and ante-post backers of Manitoulin at 33–1 had the depressing experience of seeing their now Piggott-less fancy pushed out to 50–1.

The press statement, issued in the name of Vincent O'Brien, had been tactfully worded: 'At a meeting between myself, Williamson and Roberto's owner John Galbreath, it was decided that Bill Williamson would not be in the saddle at Epsom, but it was agreed that Williamson would be back on Roberto for some future engagements. This is only a question of Williamson's fitness and there is no ill feeling involved.'

But the newspapers managed to unearth ill feeling by the bucket-load. Bill Williamson's wife Zelma called the removal of her husband 'jolly disgraceful', and the jockey himself did not mask his disgruntlement: 'A shock? It certainly was. I was not consulted about the matter. I was just told that Piggott was going to ride the horse.' Williamson's suggestion that there had been no meeting was repeated to another journalist: 'Meeting? You must be joking! I was just told that I'd lost the ride.'

The barrage of high-minded criticism came not only from the journalists. A correspondent to the *Sporting Life*, identified only as 'Disgusted' of London SW16, fulminated: 'The standard of behaviour of the owner, trainer and Piggott is little short of a scandal, and the wrath of the stewards should descend on those concerned in no uncertain manner.'

Lord Wigg, chairman of the Betting Levy Board, chimed in with his view that it was 'a disgraceful affair'.

A more measured judgement, delivered long after the smoke had cleared, came in Timeform's *Racehorses of 1972*, published early in 1973:

Roy Ullyett's Derby preview in the Daily Express, *7 June 1972.*

> The decision naturally aroused sympathy for the deposed jockey, but if the principle is accepted, as it surely must be, that an owner had a perfect right to put up anyone he wished on his horse, the law of the land and the Rules of Racing permitting, then there's not much point in criticising the owner for exercising that right. Presumably the only things that could be taken exception to were if the terms of a contract were broken or if Williamson's injury was used just as a pretext to have him substituted. In neither instance do we know this to be the case. It's no use complaining about the demise of old-fashioned values such as sportsmanship. Racing is now a business, like it or not: the difference between winning and losing the Derby nowadays could well be over a million pounds.

Opposite page:
*Pentland Firth (Pat
Eddery) leads the field
round Tattenham
Corner. Roberto (white
face) is in the middle of
the picture, with
Rheingold on his
immediate outside.*

By Derby Day attention had shifted from the musical chairs of the riding arrangements to the outcome of the race itself. Of the twenty-two runners, only Roberto and three others seemed to have any realistic chance of winning. Lyphard, trained in France by Alec Head and ridden by his son Freddy, had won the Prix Daru and appeared unlucky when fourth to Hard To Beat in the Prix Lupin. Yaroslav, trained by Noel Murless, was having his first race of the season, having won both his races as a two-year-old, the Washington Singer Stakes at Newbury (in which he beat High Top) and the Royal Lodge Stakes at Ascot. Steel Pulse had been narrowly beaten in the Craven Stakes and then dead-heated for fourth in the Two Thousand Guineas, seven and a half lengths behind the runner-up Roberto. This quartet dominated the betting market, with Roberto starting 3–1 favourite, Lyphard and Yaroslav at 4–1 and Steel Pulse at 9–1; the next horse in the market was Ormindo, winner of the Chester Vase, at 20–1. Pentland Firth, ridden by twenty-year-old Pat Eddery, was 50–1.

Among the longer-priced horses was Rheingold, trained by Barry Hills and ridden by Ernie Johnson, who had won the 1969 Derby on Blakeney. After twice finishing runner-up to Crowned Prince at two, Rheingold had opened his three-year-old campaign by winning a small race at Redcar, then finished fourth in the Blue Riband Trial Stakes at Epsom before winning the Dante Stakes at York. He started at 22–1, the same price as Scottish Rifle, who had won the Predominate Stakes at Goodwood, just beating Pentland Firth.

* * *

Pentland Firth had a reputation for being difficult at the starting stalls, but he went in fine, and made the early running at a good clip. I kept to my usual Derby plan of laying handy, not far behind the leaders. Going down into Tattenham Corner – where Freddy Head on Lyphard seemed to lose his steering completely, swinging right out into the middle of the course – we were about eighth, three or four lengths off the pace, and halfway up the straight the race had boiled down to just three runners: Pentland Firth was still leading, with Roberto challenging on his outside and Rheingold outside Roberto.

Previous pages:
*The pulsating finish of
the 1972 Derby. Lester
(quartered cap) forces
Roberto in front of
Rheingold, with
Pentland Firth well
behind in third.*

At the two-furlong marker the leading three came very close together, with Roberto, the meat in the sandwich, receiving a serious bump from Pentland Firth, who then dropped away. This left Rheingold on the outside and Roberto on his inner fighting it out, and, as so often happens with the camber in the Epsom straight, Rheingold leaned in heavily on my horse. With a furlong to go we were a neck down and I had precious little room to get after Roberto with the whip as Rheingold continued to bear down on us – then about a hundred yards out I managed to get Roberto on an even keel, and with the help of a few sharp cracks of the whip got him upsides Rheingold again. The two horses crossed the line locked together, and at first I thought we'd just been beaten – though such had been the interference from Rheingold in the last furlong that I was confident I'd get the race on an objection if the photofinish verdict went against us.

There's been a great deal of comment, on the day and ever since, about how hard I'd appeared to be on Roberto, and it can't be denied that under present-day rules regarding the use of the whip I'd have been hauled before the stewards and probably have been landed with a suspension. But such rules did not apply in 1972, and the fact is that getting after Roberto that fiercely was the only way of galvanising him. I hadn't had room to hit him earlier, and although it might have appeared that he was knuckling down to his work, I knew that he really wasn't doing a tap for me, and needed to be cajoled into making his maximum effort. This was the only Derby he'd ever run in, and I wasn't going to let him get away with dossing.

In those days photofinish verdicts took much longer than they do now, and since no one in the O'Brien camp seemed at all confident that we'd been ahead on the line, and I was convinced that we'd been beaten, I unsaddled Roberto on the course rather than take him into the winner's circle. Ernie Johnson on Rheingold did likewise. The comparative silence in which we unsaddled was interpreted in some quarters as hostility on account of the Bill Williamson business, but I was hardly going to get a rapturous reception if I didn't go into the winner's circle, and I didn't do that because at that stage I didn't know that I'd won.

As I walked back into the weighing room I heard the anouncement that a stewards' enquiry was being held, and was confident of getting the race one way or the other. After a few minutes came the result of the photofinish: Roberto by a short head (and as the official print shows, a very short head indeed). By then I was in the stewards' room with Ernie Johnson, being taken through films of the race. The more I watched that finish, the more obvious it was: Rheingold had been leaning on Roberto throughout the final furlong, and there was no way we were not going to keep the race. It took the stewards a little longer to recognise the obvious, however, and it was twenty minutes or so after the announcement of the photofinish verdict that the result of the enquiry was announced: the placings were unaltered and Roberto had won. (Manitoulin, by the way, finished eleventh.)

Bill Williamson had displayed no particular reaction one way or the other when I went back into the changing room after weighing in. He was probably too preoccupied with riding in the next race, the Woodcote Stakes. In this I rode the odds-on favourite The Go-Between, but Bill won on Captive Dream, and went on to win the last race as well. The crowd gave him a loud reception as he returned after these wins, so along with his percentage of Roberto's prize money he can't have had too bad a day after all.

∗ ∗ ∗

'COULD ANY OTHER JOCKEY HAVE DONE IT?', asked one headline on the morning after the race, a question echoed, and answered, right across the press. Whatever the rights or wrongs of the decision to remove Bill Williamson, consensus was that only Lester could have won on Roberto, given the way the race unfolded. Many papers reported seventy-four-year-old John Galbreath's vindication of the late switch: 'I thought Piggott was brilliant. He's on his own. You've got to be 100 per cent fit for this. I have a lot of experience of athletes. The baseball team I own, the Pittsburgh Pirates, has just won the World Series. I know something about fitness and I am convinced that no sportsman who has been out of action for about ten days, as Williamson was, can be 100 per cent fit. It was that factor and nothing else that brought about the switch.' Galbreath also delivered a blunt assessment of the status of the occasion: 'Anyone who doesn't consider the Epsom Derby one of the greatest sporting events in the world must be out of his mind.'

Peter Willett in the *Sporting Chronicle* described how Lester 'rode one of his greatest races' and had 'by far his toughest Derby ride', while Clive Graham in the *Daily Express* started his race report with 'The 193rd Derby Stakes goes down into history as one of the standouts in its long career – not for the quality of the field, but for the dramatic incidents leading up to it, and its fantastic outcome.' Michael Phillips in *The Times* declared that, whatever one's view of the pre-race controversy, 'no one in the mighty Derby throng could deny that we were treated to a great display of expertise and fierce race riding by the champion jockey. Piggott's uncanny skill at Epsom seems to assert itself on this, the greatest of racing occasions.' (Phillips also paid tribute to a young trainer named Barry Hills, who with Rheingold and Our Mirage saddled the runner-up and fourth horse with his first ever runners in the Derby.)

The peerless Hugh McIlvanney summed it up best on the front page of the *Daily Express*: 'When all the vitriol had been spilled, the finish had been fought, the inquiry held, and the booty divided, the one inevitable winner at Epsom yesterday was the Derby itself. It remains the greatest stayer in racing, the big one that never lets you down. And its excitement and fascination are only increased by little things like an American millionaire's willingness to slap Bill Williamson in the face in order to let Lester Piggott slap a horse called Roberto on the rump ... No jockey ever born could have ridden the bay colt better. In matters of subtlety and refinement, of balance and timing, Williamson yields to no rider, but he does not drive with the almost irresistible strength of Piggott and it was driving that Roberto required ... Roberto, who is named after Roberto Clemente, one of the biggest hitters in American baseball, could have been forgiven for thinking his namesake was on his back, complete with bat.' McIlvanney went on to quote bookmaker John Banks: 'There's so much rubbish talked about what happened over that ride. You saw the proof today in that last furlong. Old Bill is a great jockey but he couldn't have done that job. No one but Lester could.'

Shifting the attention from the winning jockey to the second-placed, a few days later John Oaksey in the *Sunday Telegraph* expressed sympathy for

Rheingold's rider: 'It would be difficult to imagine a much less desirable position than the one in which poor Ernie Johnson found himself. To have Lester Piggott beside you in any finish is doubtless bad enough, but to have him there in a Derby when your horse is hanging as violently as Rheingold was must be like waking up in bed with a hungry tiger.'

Roberto brought Lester his sixth Derby victory, equalling the record set by Jem Robinson, who won six times between 1817 and 1836 (see page 235). Steve Donoghue also rode six Derby winners between 1915 and 1925, but his initial two came during the First World War when a substitute race was run on the July Course at Newmarket. Only Robinson and Piggott had won six at Epsom.

*　*　*

I didn't ride Roberto again that season. Johnny Roe had a similar agreement with Vincent as Liam Ward had secured, and took the ride in the Irish Derby at the beginning of July, in which he started favourite but was comprehensively beaten behind Steel Pulse – ridden by none other than Bill Williamson. I came third on the second favourite Ballymore, who earlier in the year had won the Irish Two Thousand Guineas.

Roberto's next race was the Benson and Hedges Gold Cup over ten and a half furlongs at the York August meeting. The conditions of this new race were framed to set up a clash between Mill Reef and Brigadier Gerard, who had not met since the 1971 Two Thousand Guineas and both of whom had remained in training as four-year-olds. Such a contest was the cause of huge anticipation – and billed as yet another 'Race of the Century' – which collapsed when it was announced that Mill Reef would miss the race on account of a swollen hock. (This was not the injury which ended his racing career: that happened on the gallops later in August.) In Mill Reef's absence Brigadier Gerard, who by then was unbeaten in fifteen races, most recently the King George VI and Queen Elizabeth Stakes at Ascot, became a hot favourite, even though his opponents at York included Rheingold as well as Roberto.

As with all his horses, Vincent was prepared to run Roberto in this valuable new race only if all conditions were exactly right, and would not commit himself until quite close to the day of the race. So when Barry Hills asked if I would ride Rheingold, who following his narrow defeat in the Derby had been a brilliant winner of the Grand Prix de Saint-Cloud (I was third on Hard To Beat), I agreed readily. I reasoned that the flat, galloping track at York would suit this big, long-striding horse much better than Epsom, but even so I did not much fancy our chances against Brigadier Gerard.

John Galbreath brought the top-class Panamanian jockey Braulio Baeza over from the USA to ride Roberto, who started at 12–1, third favourite of the five runners behind Brigadier Gerard (1–3) and Rheingold (7–2), and on the face of it represented a very generous price. It looked even more generous after the race, as Roberto slammed out of the starting stalls like a bat out of hell and maintained a relentless gallop all the way round. Halfway up the straight Joe Mercer on Brigadier Gerard tried to get to him, but the Brigadier's effort soon petered out, and Roberto won by three lengths. He was the only horse ever to finish in front of Brigadier Gerard, who won his next two races and was then retired.

Braulio Baeza was back on Roberto in the Prix Niel at Longchamp, the horse's Arc warm-up in which I beat him a length on Hard To Beat, and in the Arc itself, when he finished seventh behind San San.

Roberto was kept in training as a four-year-old in 1973, and I rode him in all his three races. He finished runner-up to Ballymore in the Nijinsky Stakes at Leopardstown, and then on the day after the 1973 Derby returned to Epsom to win the Coronation Cup in a canter by five lengths from Attica Meli, in the process confirming my opinion that he was a much better horse on a left-handed course than a right-handed. In fact that day Roberto was the best I ever knew him, and when conditions were in his favour he was a very good horse indeed. His final race was in the King George at Ascot, where he finished eleventh of twelve as the filly Dahlia turned in an amazing six-length victory over Rheingold, ridden that day by Yves Saint-Martin. (Roberto had also been due to run in the Eclipse Stakes, run in 1973 at Kempton Park, when I was sidelined by suspension. Geoff Lewis was booked to ride, but Vincent withdrew Roberto on the morning of the race as he was not happy with the going. He was similarly withdrawn late from the 1973 Benson and Hedges Gold Cup.) There was never any intention to run Roberto in that year's Arc – which I won on Rheingold – and plans to go for the Champion Stakes at Newmarket in October were dropped when he pulled a ligament on the gallops. He was retired to stud in the USA.

Roberto had to have things his own way – which specifically meant going left-handed in top-of-the-ground conditions. Such factors didn't play his way very often, but when they did he was a champion.

* * *

Syndicated at a valuation of $3.2 million, Roberto stood as a stallion at John Galbreath's Darby Dan stud in Kentucky, where he had been born. His progeny include Sookera (from his first crop, winner of the Cheveley Park Stakes in 1977); the talented but enigmatic middle-distance horse Critique; Silver Hawk, a good racehorse and later an influential sire whose offspring included 1997 Derby winner Benny The Dip; 1979 St Leger and Irish St Leger winner Touching Wood; Robellino; Slightly Dangerous, dam of the great miler Warning; At Talaq, winner of the 1986 Melbourne Cup; Bob Back; Lear Fan; Celestial Storm; Sunshine Forever and Kris S sire of 2003 Derby winner Kris Kin. Casual Look, winner of the 2003 Oaks, also has Roberto as a grandsire, through her sire and his son Red Ransom.

Notoriously difficult to keep placid at stud, Roberto died at the age of nineteen in August 1988 after sustaining head injuries while alone in his box at Darby Dan, just two weeks after the death of his owner John Galbreath at the age of ninety.

Roberto was Lester's narrowest Derby winner, and his defeat of Rheingold provided one of the most frenetically exciting finishes in the history of the race. But unfortunately the 1972 Derby is destined to be remembered above all for the rumpus surrounding riding plans. Bill Williamson, who never rode a Derby winner, died in Melbourne in January 1979 at the early age of fifty-six

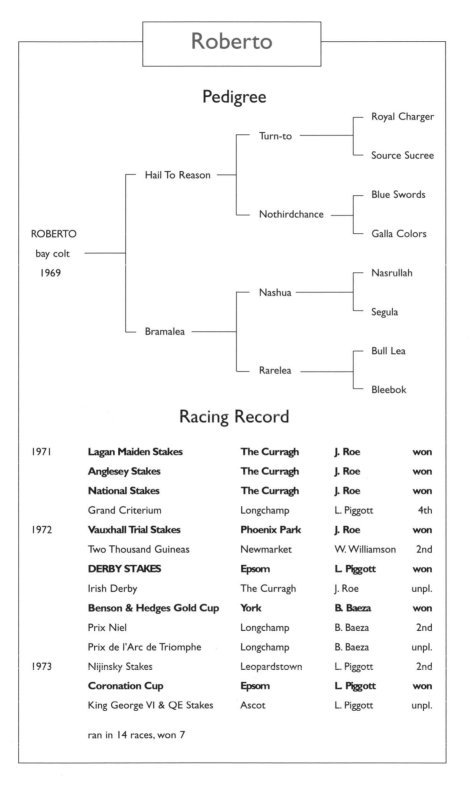

Roberto

Pedigree

ROBERTO
bay colt
1969

- Hail To Reason
  - Turn-to
    - Royal Charger
    - Source Sucree
  - Nothirdchance
    - Blue Swords
    - Galla Colors
- Bramalea
  - Nashua
    - Nasrullah
    - Segula
  - Rarelea
    - Bull Lea
    - Bleebok

Racing Record

Year	Race	Course	Jockey	Result
1971	**Lagan Maiden Stakes**	**The Curragh**	**J. Roe**	**won**
	Anglesey Stakes	**The Curragh**	**J. Roe**	**won**
	National Stakes	**The Curragh**	**J. Roe**	**won**
	Grand Criterium	Longchamp	L. Piggott	4th
1972	**Vauxhall Trial Stakes**	**Phoenix Park**	**J. Roe**	**won**
	Two Thousand Guineas	Newmarket	W. Williamson	2nd
	DERBY STAKES	**Epsom**	**L. Piggott**	**won**
	Irish Derby	The Curragh	J. Roe	unpl.
	Benson & Hedges Gold Cup	**York**	**B. Baeza**	**won**
	Prix Niel	Longchamp	B. Baeza	2nd
	Prix de l'Arc de Triomphe	Longchamp	B. Baeza	unpl.
1973	Nijinsky Stakes	Leopardstown	L. Piggott	2nd
	Coronation Cup	**Epsom**	**L. Piggott**	**won**
	King George VI & QE Stakes	Ascot	L. Piggott	unpl.

ran in 14 races, won 7

Opposite page:
Roberto at the Darby Dan Stud in Kentucky with his groom Floyd Wilson, 1979.

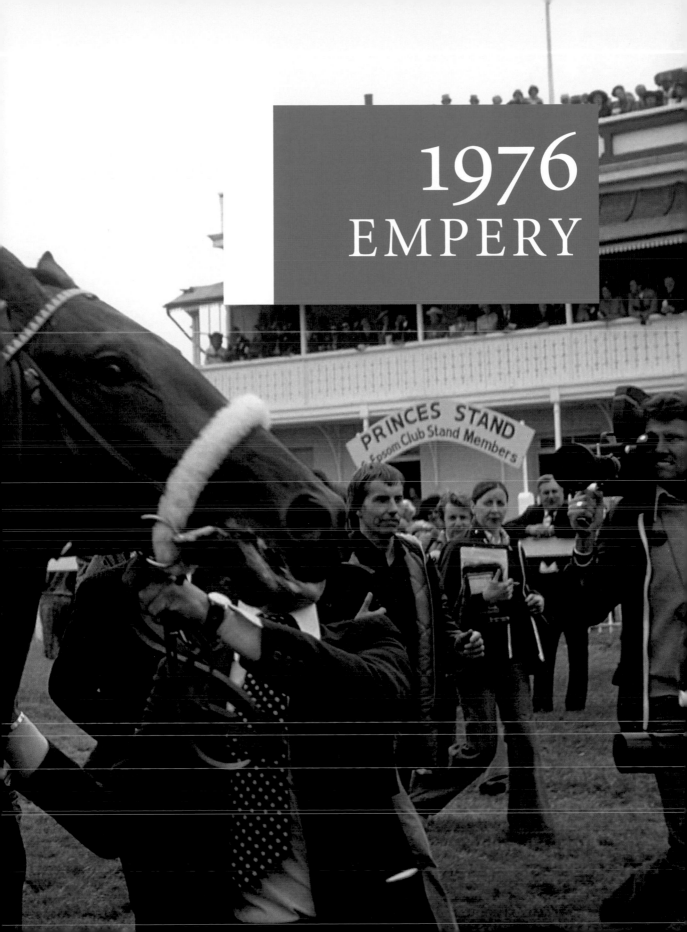

1976
EMPERY

Previous pages:
Seven up: Lester returns
after winning the 1976
Derby on Empery.

197th Derby Stakes

2 June 1976
going: good
£111,825.50 to winner

1	**EMPERY**	**L. Piggott**	**10–1**
2	RELKINO	J. Mercer	25–1
3	OATS	Pat Eddery	10–1
4	HAWKBERRY	C. Roche	100–1
5	Wollow	G. Dettori	11–10 fav
6	Vitiges	G. Rivases	16–1
7	No Turning	A. Murray	25–1
8	Smuggler	F. Durr	45–1
9	Danestic	E. Hide	50–1
10	Radetzky	M. Thomas	100–1
11	Tierra Fuego	W. Carson	35–1
12	Norfolk Air	R. Hutchinson	10–1
13	Il Padrone	B. Rouse	150–1
14	Frankie	E. Johnson	75–1
15	Whistling Deer	G. Curran	75–1
16	Coin Of Gold	R. Fox	150–1
17	Loosen Up	G. Starkey	70–1
18	Illustrious Prince	Y. Saint-Martin	16–1
19	Kafue Park	B. Taylor	100–1
20	Phleez	T. Cain	200–1
21	Our Anniversary	E. Eldin	200–1
22	Black Sabbath	C. Leonard	100–1
23	Riboboy	G. Lewis	33–1

23 ran
distances: 3 lengths, head
time: 2 minutes 35.69 seconds
Winner bred and owned by Nelson Bunker Hunt,
trained at Chantilly by Maurice Zilber

After three winners in five runnings of the Derby, Lester could not quite reach the winner's circle again in 1973 – though on Cavo Doro he came very close. Cavo Doro was not only ridden by Lester: he was also bred by him, the outcome of Raymond Guest's invitation to Lester to send a mare to Sir Ivor during the 1968 Derby winner's first season at stud. A fine-looking bay colt out of Lester's mare Limuru, Cavo Doro was sold as a foal and then sold again at the 1971 yearling sales to Captain Marcos Lemos, owner of Petingo. As a two-year-old Cavo Doro was trained by Lester's father-in-law Sam Armstrong to win one of his four races and finish runner-up in two more (ridden in all four by Lester). This was not form which suggested he might reach the frame in the Derby, but after being transferred to Vincent O'Brien's stable during the winter he won

The finish of the 1973 Derby: Lester and Cavo Doro go down by half a length to Edward Hide and Morston.

two good races at The Curragh, the Ballymoss Stakes and the Royal Whip, and was then trained for Epsom. Cavo Doro started at 12–1 in an open-looking Derby – Ksar was 5–1 favourite, with shock Two Thousand Guineas winner Mon Fils second choice at 11–2 – and very nearly made Lester the first rider/breeder of a Derby winner.

Morston, who had raced only once before in his life and was never to race again, took the lead with over a furlong to go and ran on stoutly, repelling the persistent challenge of Cavo Doro to win by half a length on ground which was probably firmer than the runner-up would have liked. Cavo Doro was then beaten into third in the Blandford Stakes at The Curragh and finished tenth of thirteen when favourite for the St Leger. He was then retired to stud.

Early in the 1974 season there had seemed to be a serious Derby candidate at Ballydoyle in Apalachee, who had been a phenomenal two-year-old: in the *Observer*, Hugh McIlvanney wrote a glowing tribute to the colt which included the observation that 'if he ever develops a taste for pigeon pie he will be able to catch his own dinner on the wing.' But despite such notices Apalachee could only finish third in the Two Thousand Guineas when 4–9 favourite, and attention switched to another of Vincent O'Brien's colts, Cellini. He disappointed in the Irish Two Thousand Guineas, so Lester went over to Tipperary to gallop Apalachee over ten furlongs. If he stayed the distance he might yet make Epsom, but he patently failed to do so, and that prospect was gone.

The next move in the now traditional 'What Will Lester Ride In The Derby?' game was described in Lester's own autobiography:

> Then Maurice Zilber, the volatile Egyptian-born but French-based trainer whose major patron was the American oil magnate Nelson Bunker Hunt, phoned to offer me the Derby ride on Mr Hunt's Mississippian. Naturally I accepted, though I knew perfectly well that the horse was usually the ride of Bill Pyers, and that Bill would be none too pleased to find himself removed. Nor was he, and over the next few days the papers were full of his threats – which included blowing up Mr Hunt's oil wells and, much more serious, giving me a black eye. To add fuel to the fire, Maurice preposterously denied approaching me at all, which put me in an extremely bad light.

Maurice then performed a U-turn and confessed that he had indeed approached me about riding Mississippian, but said that he would also be running Blue Diamond in the race, and Bill would ride that colt. Then yet another twist: Zilber again denied my engagement for the Derby – and finally Bunker Hunt announced that he did not want Mississippian to run in the Derby at all: the horse would go for the Prix du Jockey-Club at Chantilly four days later, and Bill Pyers would ride him! … I have to say that Maurice Zilber could be downright impossible in the matter of riding plans: you never knew for sure that you were riding his horse until you got up on it in the paddock – and even then it would not have surprised me to find another jockey up there.

In the event the 1974 Derby brought Lester his first Derby runner for trainer Henry Cecil, with whom he would form such a close bond later in his career. Arthurian had not run as a two-year-old, and went to Epsom with only two outings under his belt, both maiden races at Newbury: unplaced in April when ridden by Greville Starkey, and a winner in May when ridden by Lester. The best that could be said of Arthurian was that he showed promise: he started at 28–1 in the Derby, but made little show.

Bruni, Charles St George's grey colt whom Lester partnered in 1975, had run just once as a two-year-old, unplaced in a humble maiden race at Warwick in August 1974. At three he finished runner-up in a maidens-at-closing event at Sandown Park, then won a maiden at Salisbury and was short-headed by No Alimony in the Predominate Stakes at Goodwood. Not long before the Derby, Lester was contacted by Maurice Zilber and asked if he would ride the filly Nobiliary, on whom he had won the Prix Saint-Alary at Longchamp. Running a filly in the Derby rather than the Oaks was highly unorthodox – 'I have to admit that I thought Maurice had finally gone mad' was Lester's view – and he opted to stick with Bruni. Nobiliary, ridden by Yves Saint-Martin, ran an outstanding race to finish runner-up to Grundy and Pat Eddery, while Bruni finished in the rear. There was no doubting, however, that Bruni was an immature horse at the time of the 1975 Derby, and he showed his true mettle later in the season: ridden by Tony Murray, he won the St Leger by ten lengths from Lester on King Pellinore.

For all the shenanigans with Mississippian and Nobiliary, Lester did enjoy big-race success for Nelson Bunker Hunt and Maurice Zilber in 1974 and 1975 – notably on Dahlia in the 1974 King George VI and Queen Elizabeth Stakes and 1975 Benson and Hedges Gold Cup – and in 1976 finally wore the Hunt colours (light and dark green check, light green sleeves, white cap) in the Derby.

Bred in the USA by his owner, Empery was a son of Vaguely Noble (in whom Hunt had a half share and who had beaten Sir Ivor in the 1968 Arc) out of a Derby-winning mare: Pamplona II won fourteen races in Peru, including the Derby Nacional. Her progeny before Empery included the filly Pampered Miss, who won the Poule d'Essai des Pouliches (French equivalent of the One Thousand Guineas) in 1970.

Empery had shown reasonable form as a two-year-old without setting the Seine on fire. He did not run until September 1975, when he won a maiden race at Longchamp, and then moved into top-class company when finishing unplaced in the Grand Criterium at the same course the following month, winding up his juvenile campaign with a third to Arctic Tern in the Prix Thomas Bryon at Saint-Cloud. In the official ranking of the top French two-year-olds of 1975 he was rated sixteenth.

* * *

I rode Empery for the first time in the Poule d'Essai des Poulains – French Two Thousand Guineas – over one mile at Longchamp, and we finished fourth to Red Lord. He could only finish fifth in his next race, the Prix Daphnis over nine furlongs at Evry, when ridden by Freddy Head, and at that stage he did not strike me as a possible Derby winner, though given his breeding he would certainly not be seen at his best until he raced over longer distances.

On form Empery was a fair way behind his stable companion Youth, who had won the Prix Greffulhe and Prix Daru, and when the two horses met in the Prix Lupin over ten and a half furlongs at Longchamp, Youth won handily by three quarters of a length from Arctic Tern, with Empery, ridden by Bill Pyers, a length further back in third. I rode a horse called Yule Log in that race, and when the following week it was decided that Vincent's colt Malinowski, who had had a slight setback after winning the Craven Stakes, could not be got ready for the Derby I accepted an offer to ride Empery. To finish within two lengths of Youth was significantly better form than he had shown earlier in the season, and with his stable companion being aimed at the Prix du Jockey-Club he had a decent, if not an obvious chance.

The announcement that I was going to ride Empery at Epsom caused a minor eruption of indignation from those who thought he was Bill Pyers's ride, but unlike with the Mississippian episode two years earlier Bill himself did not seem unduly put out, and this time Nelson Bunker Hunt's oil wells and my features seemed not to be under threat.

In any case, neither Empery nor any other Derby candidate except one seemed to have much prospect of actually winning the race, the exception being Wollow, who had been hot favourite since winning the Two Thousand Guineas at the end of April.

Wollow went into the Derby unbeaten in six races. Trained by Henry Cecil (who was at that time established at Marriott Stables on Hamilton Road, Newmarket, though he was scheduled to move into Warren Place when Noel Murless retired at the end of the 1976 season), Wollow had won all four of his races as a two-year-old in 1975, notably the Champagne Stakes at Doncaster and the Dewhurst Stakes at Newmarket. I had finished runner-up in the latter on Malinowski, owned by Charles St George and widely regarded as the best two-year-old in Ireland that year. In the Free Handicap, the official ranking of the season's two-year-olds, Wollow was rated five pounds clear of the second horses, Hittite Glory and Wollow's stable companion Take Your Place.

In spring 1976 Wollow won the Greenham Stakes at Newbury and started even money in the Two Thousand Guineas. Ridden as in all his races to date by Gianfranco Dettori – Frankie's father – Wollow took the lead about a furlong out and ran on well to win by one and a half lengths from the French-trained colt Vitiges.

As far as the Derby was concerned, the key question was whether Wollow would stay the distance. He was a son of Wolver Hollow,

Opposite page:
*Lester and Empery in
the pre-race parade.
Behind them is Frankie
(Ernie Johnson), who
finished fourteenth.*

whose biggest moment came when I won the Eclipse Stakes over ten furlongs on him in 1969, and there was plenty of stamina in his dam's breeding. Furthermore, his manner of racing suggested that he would last the twelve furlongs at Epsom, as he was not brilliantly speedy throughout a race, in the manner of a sprinter, but needed to be pushed into his finishing effort. Timeform's *Racehorses of 1975*, assessing the matter when reviewing Wollow's two-year-old season, was in no doubt: 'Wollow is going to stay … Should Wollow beat Manado [the top French two-year-old in 1975, who was to run unplaced at Newmarket] and win the Two Thousand Guineas, the Derby, barring accidents, will be as good as over. For Wollow will be much more of an effective force at a mile and a half.'

So while Empery was a nice colt, a free-going type of horse who moved very well and was unlikely to be inconvenienced by the contours of the Derby course, I did not seriously expect him to beat the favourite, and said so on the day before the Derby in a column in the London *Evening Standard*. The headline expressed my view pretty accurately: 'I WILL NEED A GUN TO STOP WOLLOW FROM WINNING'.

* * *

That the 1976 Derby seemed to be a one-horse race was underlined by the betting market. Wollow went off at 11–10 (the shortest-priced Derby favourite since Sir Ivor in 1968), with three of his rivals on 10–1: Empery, Norfolk Air (who had won the Lingfield Derby Trial after refusing to race in the Classic Trial at Sandown) and Oats (who had finished second to Malinowski and Lester in the Craven Stakes and had then won the Blue Riband Trial at Epsom). Illustrious Prince, second in the Wood Ditton Stakes for unraced three-year-olds at Newmarket and then winner of the Glasgow Stakes at York, started at 16–1, along with Vitiges, runner-up to Wollow in the Guineas. Relkino – owned by Lady Beaverbrook, trained by Dick Hern and ridden by Joe Mercer – had won the Two Thousand Guineas Trial at Ascot but finished unplaced behind Wollow in the Two Thousand Guineas; he started at 25–1 for the Derby. There were twenty-three runners.

*   *   *

Gianfranco Dettori had never ridden at Epsom before, so to get a feel for the place before Wollow's Derby he rode Fool's Mate for Henry Cecil in the Daily Mirror Handicap over a mile and a quarter, the race immediately before the Derby. He had a bit of a baptism of fire, encountering interference inside the final furlong – an occupational hazard on this course, with tired horses reacting to the camber – and finished only fourth of seven runners. This can't have done much for his confidence, but in any case I knew that, as far as I was concerned, the key to the race was simply to beat Wollow. Vitiges made much of the early running, and it was easy enough to get Empery up into the leading group: by the top of the hill he was fourth, and I was able to nip him across to the rail and stay very handy all the way down. Vitiges still led at Tattenham Corner, with Radetzky and Relkino on his outside and Empery enjoying a smooth run in fourth. Empery did not have a change of gear in the manner of Sir Ivor or Nijinsky, so in order to stretch Wollow I had to set sail for home as soon as possible once we were into the straight. Two furlongs out Vitiges finally weakened and Relkino took the lead, with Empery giving chase. There was still no sign of Wollow, but I knew that he wouldn't be far behind.

A furlong out Empery, under strong pressure, collared Relkino and went clear, and kept going so well that at the line he was three lengths to the good, with Oats coming from out of the pack to finish third. Hawkberry, a 100–1 shot trained in Ireland by Paddy Prendergast and ridden by Christy Roche, came from behind to take fourth place, with Wollow keeping on at one pace to finish fifth. When I saw a film of the race later it seemed obvious that Wollow simply hadn't stayed the trip, though apparently he had a very bad passage from the top of the hill, which didn't help.

Empery was led into the winner's enclosure by Nelson Bunker Hunt's daughter Betsy, who at that time had taken time off from her studies in America to go on a European tour and had travelled to Epsom from Amsterdam. Her father and mother were at home in Texas, celebrating their twenty-fifth wedding anniversary. Nelson

*Opposite page:
The 1976 finish.
Empery goes clear of
Relkino (Joe Mercer,
green cap) and Oats
(Pat Eddery, quartered
cap). Hawkberry
(Christy Roche, blue
cap) is fourth, with the
favourite Wollow
(Gianfranco Dettori) on
the outside in fifth.*

Empery is led into the winner's circle by Betsy Hunt, daughter of owner Nelson Bunker Hunt.

Bunker Hunt's wife had arranged the anniversary party without realising that it was on Derby Day.

* * *

Press reaction to the unexpected victory of Empery was divided between soaring praise for the winning jockey and examination of what had happened to Wollow, and some journalists seemed to take an inappropriate delight in the misery of Gianfranco Dettori. In the *Daily Express*, James Lawton described how 'the little Italian, a tragic, broken figure, stood saying, "This is the worst moment of my life."' Others noted the anguish of

Wollow's young trainer Henry Cecil, unaware that he, unlike the jockey, would experience plenty of Derby glory in the future.

On a happier note, Peter O'Sullevan in the *Express* wrote: 'All credit to Lester for yet another superlative exhibition of Epsom sang-froid and to fifty-year-old Zilber on realising a 35–year-old dream. Born in Cairo, the son of a French father and Turkish mother, Maurice, who started training in Egypt at the age of twenty, related after his greatest triumph that "I had dreamed of training the winner of an English Derby since I was fifteen."'

But the centre of attention was Lester. James Lawton wrote that 'Piggott stood alone as the king of Epsom, a man who in his forty-first year still explores the outer reaches of professional perfection. His nerve and judgement, which long ago entered the legends of racing, have never been seen in such dramatic clarity.' Peter Willett in the *Sporting Chronicle* declared that 'Piggott's coolness and mastery of the technique of riding over one of the world's most difficult courses has finally established him the greatest rider of all time at Epsom.' The *Financial Times* applauded Lester for 'riding a typically cool and nerveless race'. Michael Phillips in *The Times* wrote: 'Piggott has long been regarded as a genius when it comes to race riding around Epsom – not that he is bad anywhere else, come to think of it! – and yesterday he rode the Classic course in a classical manner, the way he had ridden it so often in the past.'

In his *Horse and Hound* column the following weekend, John Oaksey paid further tribute: 'The icy confidence which has always been one of Lester's most priceless qualities has the effect, at Epsom on Derby Day, of turning what is, for other men, a complex and nerve-wracking occasion into an ordinary job of work.'

The same weekend Brough Scott filed for the *Sunday Times* a long post-Derby piece which began with the reaction of Empery's trainer to Lester's *Evening Standard* preview of the race:

> Maurice Zilber sat in his hotel room on Derby eve and read the evening newspaper. He saw Lester Piggott's column headlined: I Will Need a Gun to Stop Wollow. He reached for the phone, and when the silence at the other end indicated that the Epsom maestro was on the line, Zilber said: 'Looka Lester, thissa Wollow he no wonder horse. My horse, he cumma good. You needa no gun tomorrow, thissa Empery he going to win.

According to the Zilber script, Lester replied: 'Well, you are probably right – as usual.' But whatever Piggott's reservations on Derby Day, he at least knew that he was going out to do battle on an animal primed for the big time by a master of his craft ...

If the horse was primed, so too was Piggott – to a mental and physical peak extraordinary even by his own towering standards. For the Derby really does mean a lot to Lester. You see it among the mementoes at his home, you find it among the six Derby-winning jockeys in his blood and you couldn't miss it in his radiant, boyish victory mood at Epsom on Wednesday ...

After several years of close association with Piggott, who is now forty, I am sure that the gunfighter analogy suits him best. From a very early age – he rode his first winner at twelve – he has been able to do this one thing supremely well to make his way in the world. It is fired by a wild hunger for winners that drives him to take on anyone to get to the top. On the way, the wildness has sometimes spilled over, but it has always been tempered by a ferocious gunman's discipline which knows that only the steadiest hand shoots straight.

But for all the extensive coverage of a great riding record, the key quote from the 1976 Derby was a trademark Piggott response in the post-race interview. 'When did you know you'd won?', he was asked. His reply: 'Last night.'

Empery's victory at Epsom was the first leg of a Derby double for Nelson Bunker Hunt and Maurice Zilber, as four days later Youth, ridden by Freddy Head, won the Prix du Jockey-Club at Chantilly. Lester finished unplaced on Aberdeen Park.

* * *

I next rode Empery in the Irish Sweeps Derby at The Curragh at the end of June. He started odds-on but was easily beaten by another French-trained colt, Malacate, trained by Francois Boutin and ridden by Philippe Paquet, who had run third to Youth in the Prix du Jockey-Club. Empery took up the running coming into the straight, but had no answer when Malacate challenged a furlong and a half out. He simply couldn't quicken, and was beaten two and a half lengths.

The Irish Derby proved to be Empery's last race. The intention was to train him for the Benson and Hedges Gold Cup at York, but he missed that race on account of a slight injury, and in autumn 1976 was sent to the USA for the Man o'War Stakes at Belmont Park. But he missed that race as well – reportedly he had lost a great deal of condition while in quarantine – and was retired to stud in Kentucky.

I suppose that in terms of his overall record Empery has to be rated the worst of my nine Derby winners. He won only two races, and there's no doubt that the standard of the 1976 field was not very high. But all Derby winners are good on the day, and Empery has a special place in my affections as the horse who brought me my seventh Derby, more than any other jockey in the history of the race. Although as a rule I'm not especially bothered about statistics and records, I have to admit that I took special satisfaction from that landmark.

* * *

Empery and Youth both stood as stallions at Gainesway Farm, one of the principal studs in Kentucky. They were syndicated as a pair, members of the syndicate each paying $300,000 for a share in both horses and thereby buying an entitlement to one nomination per year to each horse. In 1984 Empery was sold to Japan, where he stood at the Symboli Stud. In December that year he renewed acquaintance with his Epsom partner when Lester visited the stud after riding Strawberry Road in the Japan Cup.

The Derby class of 1976 was considered no better than average in the opinion of most form experts, but several of the beaten horses went on to win important races.

Wollow was returned to shorter distances in the ten-furlong Eclipse Stakes in July. Starting 9–4 favourite and ridden by Gianfranco Dettori despite post-Derby speculation that he might lose the ride, he was easily beaten by the Francois Boutin-trained Trepan, going down by two lengths. But the winner's post-race dope test showed traces of the banned substance theobromine and Trepan was disqualified, the race being awarded to Wollow. (Trepan was also stripped of first prize after winning the Prince of Wales's Stakes at Royal Ascot.) Wollow then won the Sussex Stakes over one mile at Goodwood and the Benson and Hedges Gold Cup over ten and a half furlongs at York before ending his career running unplaced in the Champion Stakes.

Winner of that Champion Stakes, possibly the best middle-distance race run in England in 1976, was Vitiges, sixth in the Derby, who had been transferred in the meantime from France to the Lambourn stable of Peter Walwyn. Vitiges stayed in training in 1977 but was beaten in all his three races. Relkino, runner-up to Empery, did not win later in the 1976 season but was kept in training in 1977, and connections were rewarded with two big-race victories – the Lockinge Stakes at Newbury and the Benson and Hedges Gold Cup. Oats, third in the Derby, ran fourth behind Crow in the 1976 St Leger and in 1977 won all his three races, including the Jockey Club Stakes at Newmarket and the Ormonde Stakes at Chester. He sustained a leg injury while being trained for the Coronation Cup and was retired to stud, where he became a prominent sire of jumpers. Later in the 1976 season Hawkberry won the Great Voltigeur Stakes at York, and Smuggler, ninth at Epsom, won the Princess of Wales's Stakes at the Newmarket July Meeting and the Gordon Stakes at Goodwood (beating Oats a short head).

But for all the debates about the merits of the runners in the race, the 1976 Derby has its place in racing history on account of the record set by the winning rider. In his *Daily Telegraph* report of the race, John Oaksey wrote:

> The Epsom Derby has always been an acid test of jockeys as well as horses, and yesterday Lester Piggott passed it superbly for a record-breaking seventh time. Empery's speed and courage won the prize for France and America but it was for the icy precision of his rider that the race will always be remembered ... There was never a moment when Empery occupied a less than perfect position. Always poised among the first half dozen, he did not have to check or alter course for a single stride ... All the undignified jostling for Lester Piggott's services which so often precedes Europe's most important races is entirely justified and understandable. He does not talk nearly as much or as loudly as Muhammad Ali but he, just as much as the heavyweight champion, is indeed the greatest.

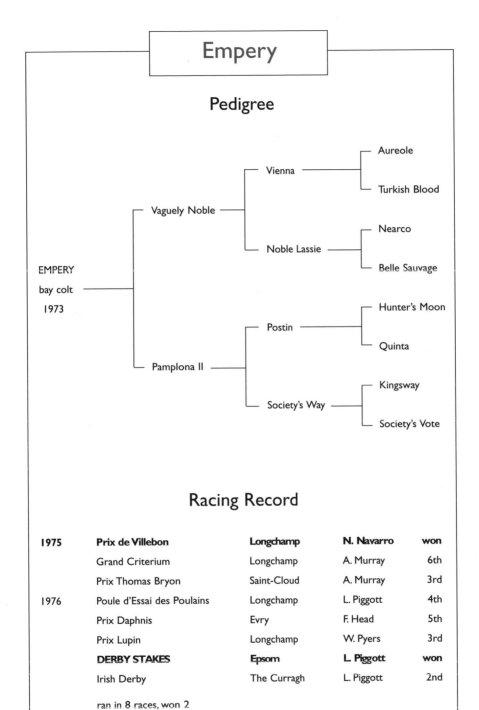

Empery

Pedigree

EMPERY
bay colt
1973

- Vaguely Noble
  - Vienna
    - Aureole
    - Turkish Blood
  - Noble Lassie
    - Nearco
    - Belle Sauvage
- Pamplona II
  - Postin
    - Hunter's Moon
    - Quinta
  - Society's Way
    - Kingsway
    - Society's Vote

Racing Record

1975	**Prix de Villebon**	**Longchamp**	**N. Navarro**	**won**
	Grand Criterium	Longchamp	A. Murray	6th
	Prix Thomas Bryon	Saint-Cloud	A. Murray	3rd
1976	Poule d'Essai des Poulains	Longchamp	L. Piggott	4th
	Prix Daphnis	Evry	F. Head	5th
	Prix Lupin	Longchamp	W. Pyers	3rd
	DERBY STAKES	**Epsom**	**L. Piggott**	**won**
	Irish Derby	The Curragh	L. Piggott	2nd

ran in 8 races, won 2

1977
THE
MINSTREL

198th Derby Stakes

1 June 1977
going: good
£107,530 to winner

1	**THE MINSTREL**	L. Piggott	5–1
2	HOT GROVE	W. Carson	15–1
3	BLUSHING GROOM	H. Samani	9–4 fav
4	MONSEIGNEUR	P. Paquet	20–1
5	Lordedaw	Y. Saint-Martin	40–1
6	Nebbiolo	G. Curran	12–1
7	Pampapaul	G. Dettori	33–1
8	Milliondollarman	G. Starkey	50–1
9	Caporello	E. Eldin	28–1
10	Valinsky	G. Lewis	20–1
11	Be My Guest	E. Hide	22–1
12	St Petersburg	P. Waldron	66–1
13	Milverton	C. Roche	33–1
14	In Haste	J. Lowe	100–1
15	Lucky Sovereign	M. Thomas	12–1
16	Gairloch	B. Taylor	33–1
17	Baudelaire	F. Durr	50–1
18	Mr Music Man	P. Cook	150–1
19	Sultan's Ruby	E. Johnson	200–1
20	Royal Plume	J. Mercer	22–1
21	Noble Venture	R. Fox	150–1
p.u.	Night Before	Pat Eddery	28–1

22 ran
distances: neck, 5 lengths
time: 2 minutes 36.44 seconds
Winner bred by E. P. Taylor, owned by Robert Sangster,
trained at Ballydoyle, County Tipperary, by Vincent O'Brien

n 1973, the year after Roberto had given him his fourth Derby victory in the eleven runnings since 1962, Vincent O'Brien purchased a two-thirds share in the Coolmore Stud, not far from Ballydoyle, and in 1975 brought in John Magnier, the young owner of the nearby Castle Hyde Stud, to run the operation. Magnier was also joint owner of the Sandville Stud with Robert Sangster, whose considerable fortune had come through his family's ownership of Vernon's Pools. Sangster, who died in April 2004, had long been a passionate devotee of racing – the first winner in his colours had been Eric Cousins-trained Chalk Stream at Haydock Park in 1960, when Sangster was twenty-four – and in the early 1970s was determined to enter the big time of bloodstock breeding. In 1975 he joined O'Brien, Magnier (who had married O'Brien's daughter Susan) and others to form a syndicate which would breed and race horses which would be trained by O'Brien. Those who had shown sufficient calibre on the racecourse would be established as stallions to breed future champions, who would themselves stand as stallions to breed the next generation, and so on.

Potentially this was very big business, and to capitalise on the international dimension which Sangster recognised as the main force in racing at the time, the syndicate knew it had to concentrate on American bloodlines. Sir Ivor, Nijinsky and Roberto were all American-bred, as was another of the great Derby winners of that time, Mill Reef, and the USA was clearly the place to buy horses which would attract international breeders.

The Coolmore-based syndicate duly made its first major foray into the American bloodstock business at the Keeneland Sales in Kentucky in July 1975. The achievements of Nijinsky five years earlier had made the progeny of Northern Dancer highly sought after, as was attested by the rise in his stud fee from $10,000 in 1966, the year that Nijinsky was conceived, to $25,000 in 1971.

At the 1975 sales the yearling which particularly caught Vincent O'Brien's eye was a chestnut colt by Northern Dancer out of the broodmare Fleur, a daughter of Nijinsky's dam Flaming Page – thus a three-parts brother to Nijinsky and, like the 1970 Triple Crown winner, bred by E. P. Taylor, though this colt had been foaled not in Canada but at the new base of Windfields Farm in Maryland.

The colt seemed to have two drawbacks: his colouring and his size. He had four white stockings in addition to a large white blaze down his face, and that amount of white is a major disincentive for many horse-buyers. The tradition of being wary of too much white on a horse's leg goes back a long way and for some experts is not just an old wives' tale: O'Brien himself thought that white about a horse's leg might signify weakness, and therefore a susceptibility to injury. The chestnut colt's size was another drawback. Unlike his distinguished close relative Nijinsky, a large and imposing horse, this fellow was very small: 'Jesus! I've got a Labrador who's only a bit bigger!', exclaimed Vincent's brother Phonsie, one of the Coolmore contingent at the sales.

It would have been easy to reject this young horse as a possible purchase, but there was something about him – in his eye, in his appearance, in the way he moved – which appealed to O'Brien, who kept returning to the colt's box for another look. Vincent himself related later: 'I was definitely concerned about his height. I remember going back to his box more than once to see if I could make myself feel any easier about it. But he was certainly small. He did grow in the end. He finished just short of 15.3 hands. But again, this Northern Dancer breed was something new in the racehorse world. They don't have to be big to be good.' (A notable example of that last statement was Northern Dancer himself, who had not reached 15.2 hands when winning his two legs of the US Triple Crown.)

The chestnut colt was bought by the bloodstock agent Tom Cooper on behalf of the Coolmore team for $200,000, and along with eleven other yearlings bought at the sale – one of them the subsequent Eclipse Stakes winner Artaius – arrived at Ballydoyle a few weeks later.

The Minstrel – as the flashy chestnut colt was named – was given plenty of time to mature and grow, and first ran as a two-year-old in the Moy Stakes at The Curragh in September 1978. Ridden by Tommy Murphy, he started at 4–9 and won by five lengths. Seventeen days later, ridden for the first time by Lester (who also rode him in all his subsequent races), he won the Larkspur Stakes at Leopardstown, starting at 4–11. He was then sent over to Newmarket for the Dewhurst Stakes, which had been won by three Derby winners of the 1970s: Nijinsky, Mill Reef and Grundy. Whether The Minstrel would go on to emulate this trio was a matter for some debate after the 1976 running. Starting at 6–5, he won easily enough by four lengths from the second favourite Saros, but the overall quality of the Dewhurst field was not, by the standards of the race, high.

Timeform's *Racehorses of 1976* looked at The Minstrel's breeding for a clue about his Derby prospects, and remained unconvinced: 'Judging from his pedigree, we should say that there is no room for doubt that The Minstrel will stay a mile and a quarter, but that it is by no means certain that he will stay a mile and a half. In which case the Two Thousand Guineas would seem the race most likely to provide him with success in a Classic. Granted normal luck in running, The Minstrel will be hard to beat at Newmarket.'

In the Free Handicap published in late November, The Minstrel was ranked joint fourth-best two-year-old of 1976, rated eight pounds below J. O. Tobin, a brilliant colt trained by Noel Murless and ridden by Lester to win his first three races, including the Richmond Stakes at Goodwood and Champagne Stakes at Doncaster, before being beaten into third in the Grand Criterium at Longchamp by the Aga Khan's Blushing Groom. Noel Murless retired at the close of the 1976 season, and J. O. Tobin was sent to the USA to continue his racing career there, so he was removed from the Classic picture.

* * *

I liked The Minstrel from the first moment I sat on him before the Larkspur Stakes. He was small but very tough, and his great quality – which he showed throughout his racing life, even after some very taxing races indeed – was how he just knuckled down to the job in hand. His first race in 1977 was the Two Thousand Guineas Trial at Ascot in early April – on the same day that Red Rum (whom I'd ridden in two of his races on the Flat) won his third Grand National. The going was desperately heavy and the opposition included Gairloch, who had been rated on the same mark as The Minstrel in the Free Handicap. The Minstrel started odds-on and went through the ground well enough to win quite easily. (On the same day Vincent's star filly Cloonlara, a daughter of Sir Ivor and an even hotter favourite for the One Thousand Guineas than The Minstrel was for the Two Thousand, disgraced herself in the fillies' trial race. The going was so bad that starting stalls could not be used for either of the Guineas trials, a flag start being substituted. Cloonlara broke well enough, but a false start was declared and we had to go back and start again, which put her in a very bad mood. When the starter let us go she simply planted herself and refused to budge.)

After Ascot, The Minstrel's preparation for the Two Thousand Guineas continued without a hitch, and on the day the starting prices – 6–5 The Minstrel, 12–1 bar – made it look like a one-horse race. Things did not work out like that. I kept The Minstrel covered up in the pack until making a forward move about three furlongs out. With a quarter of a mile to go I was having to work hard to get at the leaders, and a furlong out we were still in the shake-up, but he could not accelerate out of The Dip, and we finished third, beaten a length and the same distance by Nebbiolo, a 20–1 chance trained by Kevin Prendergast in Ireland (and a horse I'd ridden earlier in the season at Phoenix Park), and the co-second favourite Tachypous. (Cloonlara added to the gloom at Ballydoyle by finishing only fourth when favourite for the One Thousand Guineas.)

It was disappointing that The Minstrel had been beaten for the first time in his life, but we were hopeful of getting back on the winning trail in the Irish Two Thousand Guineas at The Curragh. Nebbiolo was among our opponents, but The Minstrel still started favourite. A furlong out he was disputing the lead with Lordedaw when Nebbiolo, challenging from behind and trying to find a gap, slammed into The Minstrel. Gianfranco Dettori on Pampapaul – trained in Ireland by Stuart Murless (Noel's brother) – found a clear run up the middle of the course and went clear. Under strong driving The Minstrel fought as hard as he could to claw the leader back, but just failed, and was beaten a short head. Nebbiolo came third.

Understandably Robert Sangster and Vincent were pretty downcast by this unlucky outcome. The Minstrel had lost the two races in his life which mattered most, and the prospect of his becoming a high-value stallion was looking highly improbable. Some time after the race Robert came to find me in the weighing room and asked what I thought about running The Minstrel in the Derby. To me the answer was obvious, even though The Minstrel had had two very hard races, and I replied: 'If you run him, I'll ride him. On decent ground, he'll win.' Later that evening Vincent asked me the same question and I gave the same answer. Vincent was not immediately convinced, as he had in mind the St James's Palace Stakes over one mile at Royal Ascot as the colt's next race, but I persuaded him that The Minstrel had all the balance needed to act round Epsom, and it was decided to go for the Derby.

Meanwhile the French colt Blushing Groom, the best two-year-old in Europe in 1976, had won both his races in 1977 – the Prix de Fontainebleau and the Poule d'Essai des Poulains – to make himself hot favourite for the Derby, though I was one of many who held the view that this son of Red God could not possibly stay one and a half miles in top-class company. Not long before the Derby it was announced that a deal had been arranged for Blushing Groom to stand at stud in Kentucky from 1978, at a valuation of $6 million.

* * *

Blushing Groom at 9–4 and The Minstrel at 5–1 were the only two horses to start the 1977 Derby at single-figure odds. Joint third favourites were Two Thousand Guineas winner Nebbiolo and Lucky Sovereign, who had won the Dante Stakes after running third in the Craven Stakes.

Lester and The Minstrel, led by his lad Tom O'Gorman, in the pre-race parade. Carrying the blanket is Vincent O'Brien's travelling head lad Gerry Gallagher.

Previous pages:
An unusual view of Tattenham Corner in 1977 – and of Lester's bottom, perfectly poised fourth from the left.

Hot Grove, fourth in the Craven, had gone on to win the Chester Vase by five lengths, ridden by Lester. He was trained by Fulke Johnson Houghton and ridden in the Derby by Willie Carson, who had been champion jockey in 1972 and 1973 and had first ridden in the Derby in Sir Ivor's year, 1968: in eight previous rides in the race Carson had never finished closer than fourth. Hot Grove started at 15–1.

Vincent O'Brien had two other runners in the race in the shape of Valinsky (20–1) and Be My Guest (22–1, winner of the Blue Riband Trial Stakes at Epsom earlier in the season and another son of Northern Dancer), while Pampapaul, who had beaten The Minstrel at The Curragh, was friendless in the betting market at 33–1.

This was the week given over to celebrations of the Silver Jubilee, marking twenty-five years of the Queen's reign, and there was not only a particular significance in 1977 to the traditional royal presence at Epsom, but an enhanced sense of Derby Day as a celebration of Britain as well as of its monarch.

* * *

For me, as for so many others, the Derby boiled down to one factor. If Blushing Groom stayed, he would win. If he didn't, he wouldn't.

The going was officially good, but when I won the opening race of the afternoon on Fire Angel it seemed to me to be running on the fast side. The Minstrel could get a little stirred up before his races and Vincent as always took no chances, stuffing cotton wool in the horse's ears before he was led into the parade ring so that he would not be put off by the unusual level of noise. But The Minstrel did not turn a hair during the preliminaries, and after he had arrived at the start quite at one with himself the earplugs were removed by Vincent's assistant John Gosden, now himself a Derby-winning trainer.

Drawn towards the inside, The Minstrel was not the quickest out of the stalls – he was habitually a little slow to get into his stride – and on the uphill stretch was further back than ideally I would have liked. Milliondollarman, a 50–1 outsider, had the lead, and I was gradually able to improve our position from the top of the hill. At Tattenham Corner the pace was still being set by Milliondollarman, but Willie

Opposite:
Lester and The Minstrel collar Willie Carson and Hot Grove. Blushing Groom (Henri Samani) is third.

Gotcha! – The Minstrel by a neck from Hot Grove.

Carson had been moving Hot Grove closer and was now in second place, with Caporello on the rail level with The Minstrel, no more than three lengths behind the leader. I was happy enough with my position, but I knew that not far behind me was Henri Samani on Blushing Groom, and until the race came to the boil no one would know for sure whether the French horse would stay or not.

Once we were in the straight Willie set Hot Grove alight and started riding him for all he was worth. He took the lead with fully three furlongs to go and ran on resolutely, with The Minstrel giving chase on his outside and Blushing Groom not far behind and closing fast. With less than two furlongs to go I sensed that Blushing Groom had reached the end of his tether, and asked The Minstrel for yet more effort. Ears flat back – his characteristic way of racing, and in his case a sign that he was giving his maximum – he stretched out his neck, stuck out his head and galloped his heart out. Now was no time to be easy on him and I went to work with the whip, but his response was fantastic, and throughout the last furlong we gradually wore down Hot Grove. With fifty yards to go it still must have looked as if Willie would hold on, but I asked The Minstrel for a little bit more and from somewhere he found it, clawing his way back in the shadow of the winning post to win by a neck. A magnificent race – and no horse I ever rode showed more unflinching courage in a finish than The Minstrel did that day.

Blushing Groom, who had patently failed to stay, finished five lengths behind Hot Grove, and his defeat caused a quick change of arrangements at Annabel's. The Aga Khan had been so confident that Blushing Groom would win that his booking for a celebration party at that fashionable Berkeley Square night club stipulated that the floral settings on each table should be in his red and green racing colours. Hardly had The Minstrel pulled up than Charles Benson, who had been writing as 'The Scout' on the *Daily Express* since Clive Graham's death in 1974, was on the phone to Annabel's to change the booking into the name of Robert Sangster and decree that the floral arrangements should be in the green, white and blue of the Sangster silks. We had a great party that night – sportingly attended by the Aga Khan himself.

* * *

The Minstrel brought Lester his eighth Derby victory, and his fifth in the last ten runnings, an extraordinary strike rate.

The Times set the tone of press reaction on the morning after the race: 'By winning the Derby on The Minstrel yesterday,' wrote Michael Phillips, 'Lester Piggott has demonstrated yet again why there has always been such

The Minstrel returns …

a clamour for his services on this particular occasion. He is a law unto himself there. And it is as simple as that.' Taking a similar line, Jim Stanford in the *Daily Mail* did not beat about the bush: 'Lester Piggott crowned a glorious career with a Jubilee gem in yesterday's Derby. He has ridden a host of great races but this win was the finest of them all … This was Piggott the Supreme at his superb best, riding at a peak seldom, if ever, reached by any other jockey – and never equalled over the tricky Epsom gradients even by the immortal Steve Donoghue'

In the *Daily Express*, Peter O'Sullevan quoted the Irish training legend Paddy Prendergast describing Lester's performance as 'One of the greatest pieces of riding I've ever seen', an estimation echoed elsewhere. In the same paper James Lawton described the victory of Lester ('of the iron hands and parchment face') as 'a win fit for a king of the Turf – and fit for a Queen in her Jubilee year.' In the *Sun*, John Trickett expressed the exasperation of the punter who had missed the obvious: 'What the hell can one say? When the biggest fish comes up from the deep to snatch the fattest bait in British racing for the eighth time, words fly up in the

sky with the Epsom Downs kites. It was, of course, Lester Piggott there yet again on these sun-baked open spaces. We all should have known. So many of us didn't ... After all our experience of the Long Fella we should have known better. When Lester is aboard on this trick-track you back Lester!'

John Oaksey in the *Daily Telegraph* acclaimed Lester's 'dedication, icy nerve and superlative horsemanship', while the *Sporting Chronicle* report by Peter Willett declared that the winning jockey 'now stands out as the greatest expert of all at riding in this most famous of races.'

Robert Sangster revealed that he and his co-owners Vincent O'Brien and the Scottish landowner Simon Fraser had declined an offer of £1 million for The Minstrel a few days before the race, and added: 'He is not for sale now, and at the end of his racing career, which may embrace a four-year-old campaign, he will retire to the Coolmore Stud in Tipperary.'

Three days later Lester donned the Sangster silks again to ride Barry Hills-trained Durtal in the Oaks, and this time disaster struck, as he described in his autobiography:

Cantering back past the stands after the parade she was pulling very hard, which caused her saddle to slip, and as we turned the bend near the entrance to the paddock the saddle went right round underneath her and I came off. Terrified, she bolted, dragging me behind her with my foot stuck in the stirrup, and headed for a fence with concrete uprights, a familiar enough feature of British racecourses before safety regulations mercifully replaced them with plastic poles. When we hit the upright the impact broke the aluminium stirrup iron, freeing my foot, but Durtal impaled herself on the splintered wood of the fence, narrowly missing puncturing a main artery. She was eventually caught and calmed down, and lived to race again, while I, a little shaken, was taken back to the ambulance room, where I recovered well enough to ride the winner of the last – Elland Road for my brother-in-law Robert Armstrong.

One way and another, for Lester it had been quite a week.

*   *   *

Considering the hard race he'd had in the Derby, The Minstrel could have been forgiven for taking a little time to recover, but such was his iron constitution that he showed no ill effects whatsoever. On his return to Ballydoyle he ate up every oat, and was soon back in the training routine, with the Irish Derby his next target.

He started 11–10 favourite at The Curragh, where he was opposed by three horses he had beaten in the Derby – fourth-placed Monseigneur (trained in France by Francois Boutin) along with Lucky Sovereign and Milverton (both of whom finished well back). He won easily – by his standards – by a length and a half from Lucky Sovereign, but had drifted across the course when under pressure in the final furlong, and we had to survive an objection from Frankie Durr on the runner-up before being confirmed the winner.

Four weeks later The Minstrel went to Ascot for the King George – the first time he faced older horses. The best four-year-olds in the race were 1976 St Leger winner Crow and Exceller, who had won the Coronation Cup the day after The Minstrel's Derby and then gone on to win the Grand Prix de Saint-Cloud. Bruni, whom I had ridden in the 1975 Derby and who had won that year's St Leger, was now five and had yet to win a race in 1977, while another five-year-old was Orange Bay, trained by Peter Walwyn and owned by Carlo Vittadini (who had won the 1975 Derby with Grundy). Orange Bay, winner of the Italian Derby in 1975, had finished a good third behind Pawneese and Bruni in the 1976 King George, but his earlier form in 1977 was less good, and he started at 20–1. Crystal Palace, winner of the Prix du Jockey-Club, was the only other three-year-old in the field. The Minstrel, who looked quite outstanding that day, having filled out considerably in the month since running at The Curragh, started 7–4 favourite, with Crow and Exceller next in the betting.

At the turn into the short Ascot straight I had The Minstrel about fifth or sixth, and when with more than a furlong to go Pat Eddery shot Orange Bay into the lead, The Minstrel went in hot pursuit. We collared Orange Bay and went half a length up inside the final furlong, but Orange Bay fought back ferociously, and we had a real hammer-and-tongs fight to the line, with The Minstrel just holding the older horse off to win by a short head. Again I could only marvel at The Minstrel's courage and tenacity, and for me this was at least as good a race as, and probably even better than, the famous King George battle between Grundy and Bustino two years earlier.

That proved to be the last race that The Minstrel ran. He was a marvellously genuine, tough and courageous little horse, and of all my nine Derby winners he had the best physique for Epsom – compact and exceptionally well balanced. I wish there'd been a few more like him.

* * *

Although Robert Sangster and John Magnier had been very keen to keep The Minstrel in Europe as a stallion and stand him at Coolmore, the power of the dollar was such that they could not resist an offer to return him to Windfields Farm in Maryland, where his breeder E. P. Taylor had constructed an offer which valued the horse at $9 million, far in excess of what could have been expected from a syndicate of European breeders. Taylor would keep a half share for himself, and knew that there would be plenty of American breeders keen to send their mares to the Derby winner.

Meanwhile The Minstrel was being trained for the 1977 Prix de l'Arc de Triomphe, and in mid August it was reported that connections were going to accept an invitation to run him against top American horses Forego and Seattle Slew in the Washington DC International on 5 November that year (which would be Lester's forty-second birthday). But scarcely had the communal mouth of the racing fraternity started to water at such a prospect than it was announced that an outbreak of equine contagious metritis in England was leading to an imminent ban on bloodstock entering the USA from Europe. In order to beat the ban The Minstrel was hastily packed off across the Atlantic, at literally a few hours' notice, and all plans for further races were abandoned.

In spring 1978 The Minstrel commenced his new duties at a fee of $50,000, a sum which had risen to $185,000 by the mid 1980s. To have passed on his ability, constitution and resolution to his progeny on a regular basis would have been too much to ask, but he had plenty of high-class offspring. His second crop produced L'Emigrant, who won the Poule d'Essai des Poulains in 1983, and his third included Palace Music, who won several good races in Europe and the USA, and beat Pebbles in the 1984 Champion Stakes. The Minstrel's first Classic winner in England was Musical Bliss in the 1989 One Thousand Guineas, while other well-known sons and daughters include Bakharoff, Minstrella, Melodist, Silver Fling, and Opening Verse, who won the Breeders' Cup Mile in 1991.

When Windfields was wound up in 1989 The Minstrel was relocated to the Overbrook Stud in Kentucky, where he was put down in September 1990 at the age of sixteen, following a bout of severe laminitis.

Two of the horses who finished behind The Minstrel at Epsom also made a significant impact at stud. After his failure to last out one and a half miles in the Derby, Blushing Groom was returned to a mile for the Prix Jacques le Marois at Deauville in August 1977: he started at 1–5 but was beaten half a length by the filly Flying Water (winner of the 1976 One Thousand Guineas) and did not run again. He was retired to the Gainesway Stud in Kentucky, where his offspring included Rainbow Quest, winner of the 1985 Prix de l'Arc de Triomphe, Al Bahathri, winner of the 1985 Irish One Thousand Guineas and Coronation Stakes, and most notably the great Nashwan, winner in 1989 of the Two Thousand Guineas, Derby, Eclipse Stakes and King George. Blushing Groom died in on Christmas day 1992.

The influence of Be My Guest on the bloodstock industry in Ireland is announced by his statue at the entrance to Coolmore Stud in Tipperary, though he had already made his mark on breeding history when in 1975 he fetched 127,000 guineas at the Goffs sale in Ireland, briefly a European record for a yearling. After finishing eleventh behind The Minstrel at Epsom he reverted to one mile, winning the Desmond Stakes at The Curragh and the Goodwood Mile, which proved his last race.

With The Minstrel departed to the USA, it fell to Be My Guest to bring Northern Dancer blood to Coolmore in 1978, and he was an immediate success. His very first crop made him champion sire for 1982, with such horses as On The House (One Thousand Guineas) and Assert (Prix du Jockey-Club, Irish Derby, Benson and Hedges Gold Cup and Joe McGrath Memorial Stakes — subsequently Irish Champion Stakes). Later progeny included Go And Go, winner of the 1990 Belmont Stakes, and Pentire, runner-up to Lammtarra in the 1995 King George VI and Queen Elizabeth Diamond Stakes and winner of that race the following year. Be My Guest did notably well as a broodmare sire: his daughter Offshore Boom is the dam of Rock Of Gibraltar, winner of a record seven successive Group One races in 2001 and 2002. When Be My Guest died at the age of thirty in February 2004 he was described in the *Racing Post* as 'one of the founding fathers of the Coolmore stallion operation'.

But what of Hot Grove, who so nearly joined the exclusive club of Derby winners? After Epsom he started favourite for the Great Voltigeur Stakes at York, but finished a remote fourth behind Ballydoyle's new star Alleged, who scorched home by seven lengths and went on to win the Arc both that season and the following year. Hot Grove then finished third to Orange Bay in the Cumberland Lodge Stakes at Ascot, and won the St Simon Stakes at Newbury. Kept in training in 1978, he kicked off the season with a straightforward victory in the Westbury Stakes at Sandown Park. He was then beaten a head by Crow in the Ormonde Stakes at Chester after a stirring battle up the straight, ran second in the Grand Prix d'Evry in France, and finished his racing career when at odds of 1–3 he finished third of four runners in the Princess of Wales's Stakes at the Newmarket July Meeting. He was syndicated at a valuation of £320,000 to stand at stud in Newmarket, but never produced any offspring of great significance.

＊　＊　＊

The 1977 Derby won by The Minstrel has a place not only in racing history but also in the history of the modern theatre. Howard Brenton set his play *Epsom Downs* on Derby Day 1977 and uses the occasion – as many other writers have done over the last two centuries – as a microcosm of English society.

Naturally Lester features a great deal throughout the play. The policeman Sergeant Blue declares that 'If Lester Piggott wins the Derby today, I will marry the Pope.' A group of young revellers adapt the National Anthem when chanting 'God save our gracious Lester / Long Live our noble Lester / God save our Lester ….' Miss Mottrom the evangelist tries to preach to the crowd – 'Lester Piggott? What horse does he ride? The Minstrel. Minstrel means singer. But what song does he sing? Not the Lord's song. Not the Lord's song …', while in the betting ring the bookies invoke the magic name to drum up business from lady racegoers: 'Come on, girls, get your money on Lester! Five to one!' … 'Lester, the housewife's fancy!' … 'Let Lester be your tipple, ladies!' During the parade, spectators crowd to get a glimpse of their fancy: 'Where's Lester? Annie, where's Lester?' 'He's not gone by yet! You'll know him, when he does. He's got an arse like a little cream bun.' A woman tells her husband that she is pregnant. 'Great,' he replies, 'If it's a boy we'll call it Lester.' 'What if it's a girl?' 'We'll call it Lesterine.'

As the field thunders down the hill, the commentary is supplied by 'The Derby', a personification of the race played by an actor. He makes an aside, 'Lester's brain ticks, like an intercontinental ballistic missile, on trajectory', and describes the final moments of the race:

> The closing stages of the 1977 Derby. Blushing Groom has nothing left. Willie Carson on Hot Grove thinks the race is his. Then Lester Piggott lets the reins slip two inches through the palms of his hands. The Minstrel responds. A bat out of hell, bullet out of a gun, the lash of a whip. A hundred yards to run in the Derby. Lester Piggott and Willie Carson. The Minstrel on the near side, Hot Grove on the far side. AND in the last second, like throwing a knife through a doorway as the door slams – The Minstrel wins.

The outcome does not please Grandpa:

Lester Piggott? Win the Derby on The Minstrel? What good's that to the working man? Five to one, less tax? No good at all. Bloody conspiracy. That Lester Piggott. That trainer from Tipperary. Got together with that man on the telly with the hat. Done the working man in, yet again. The Minstrel? Drifts to the left. Oh well. Derby done. Heavy boozing starts.

But Margaret and her husband Sandy have put all their savings on The Minstrel in the hope of winning enough to buy a house and get them out of the Dormobile where they now live, and Sandy is duly grateful:

Lester Piggott, five to one. That little bookie from the sticks I put it on with. Writhe? I had to wait nearly an hour while he called in all the money he'd laid off on me. God bless you, Lester! Wherever you are. Sipping your half glass of champagne, chewing your Ryvita biscuit.

* * *

For all the frantic excitement of the final-furlong battle with Hot Grove, the true importance of The Minstrel's victory in the 1977 Derby went far beyond the result of the race itself. For his win brought Robert Sangster and his Coolmore operation the biggest prize in world Thoroughbred breeding with the first consignment of American-bred yearlings they had bought in Kentucky in 1975, and the stakes in international breeding had been raised hugely.

When the European record of 127,000 guineas paid in 1975 for Be My Guest was demolished just a month later by the 202,000 guineas paid by Lady Beaverbrook for a yearling who would be named Million (and who unlike Be My Guest proved very moderate on the racecourse), some observers thought the breeding world had gone mad. But within a few years such a sum looked like small change. In 1983 a son of Northern Dancer was sold in Kentucky for $10.2 million: named Snaafi Dancer, he went into training with John Dunlop but never raced, and then proved similarly useless at stud. The $13.1 million paid for a Seattle Slew yearling colt in 1985 remains a record nearly two decades later.

The explosion in prices in the later 1970s and early 1980s is to a great degree the result of major bidding battles at the sales between the

Coolmore operation and the Maktoum brothers, led by Sheikh Mohammed bin Rashid al Maktoum, as both sides strove for supremacy in the world bloodstock market. Had The Minstrel and Lester not collared Hot Grove in the shadow of the Epsom winning post, the Coolmore colt would not have become unconscionably valuable, and the Sangster-led business would never have taken off in the way it did. Further, according to the American racing writer Steven Crist, 'The Minstrel's $9-million price tag certified the fashionability of the Northern Dancer line', which was crucial to the success of the Coolmore business.

The Minstrel syndicated at a valuation of $9 million – at the time about £6 million – and Hot Grove at £320,000. What a difference a neck made.

The Minstrel

Pedigree

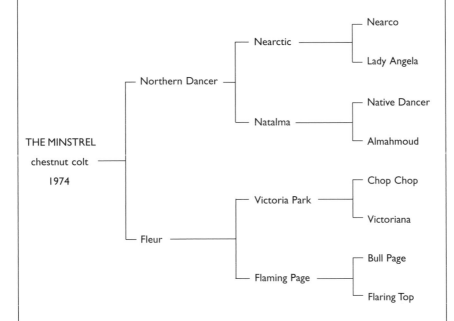

THE MINSTREL
chestnut colt
1974

- Northern Dancer
  - Nearctic
    - Nearco
    - Lady Angela
  - Natalma
    - Native Dancer
    - Almahmoud
- Fleur
  - Victoria Park
    - Chop Chop
    - Victoriana
  - Flaming Page
    - Bull Page
    - Flaring Top

Racing record

1976	**Moy Stakes**	**The Curragh**	**T. Murphy**	**won**
	Larkspur Stakes	**Leopardstown**	**L. Piggott**	**won**
	Dewhurst Stakes	**Newmarket**	**L. Piggott**	**won**
1977	**Two Thousand Guineas Trial**	**Ascot**	**L. Piggott**	**won**
	Two Thousand Guineas	Newmarket	L. Piggott	3rd
	Irish Two Thousand Guineas	The Curragh	L. Piggott	2nd
	DERBY STAKES	**Epsom**	**L. Piggott**	**won**
	Irish Derby	**The Curragh**	**L. Piggott**	**won**
	King George VI & QE Stakes	**Ascot**	**L. Piggott**	**won**

ran in 9 races, won 7

1983
TEENOSO

The DERBY STA
1 J. REID
3 M. J. KINAN
5 C. ASMUSSI
7 P. ROBINSO
9 M. MILLE
12 W. SHOEMAKE
13 G. BAXTE
14 W. CARSON
15 J. MERCE
16 B. ROUSE
19 F. HEAD

STARTING PRICES

HORSE

PRIC

1ST	9'2	14'1
2ND	15'8	6'1
3RD	9'2	9'1

204th Derby Stakes

1 June 1983
going: heavy
£165,080 to winner

1	**TEENOSO**	**L. Piggott**	**9–2 fav**
2	CARLINGFORD CASTLE	M. Kinane	14–1
3	SHEARWALK	W. R. Swinburn	18–1
4	SALMON LEAP	Pat Eddery	11–2
5	Guns Of Navarone	P. Robinson	20–1
6	Naar	J. Mercer	100–1
7	Pluralisme	F. Head	18–1
8	Morcon	W. Carson	17–2
9	Tolomeo	G. Dettori	14–1
10	Gordian	C. Asmussen	25–1
11	The Noble Player	S. Cauthen	16–1
12	Mitilini	G. Baxter	500–1
13	Neorion	B. Rouse	150–1
14	Wassl	A. Murray	10–1
15	Tivian	A. Barclay	500–1
16	Lomond	W. Shoemaker	9–1
17	Appeal To Me	J. Reid	500–1
18	Slewpy	Y. Saint-Martin	100–1
19	Holmbury	M. Miller	1000–1
20	Zoffany	G. Starkey	28–1
fell	Yawa	P. Waldron	50–1

21 ran
distances: 3 lengths, 3 lengths
time: 2 minutes 49.07 seconds
Winner bred by Eric Moller and White Lodge Stud,
owned by Eric Moller, trained at Newmarket by Geoffrey Wragg

As a measure of the extraordinary longevity of Lester Piggott's reign as king of the Derby, consider this: of the twenty jockeys who opposed him in the 1983 race, seven had not been born when Lester won on Never Say Die. His ninth and final victory on Teenoso came *twenty-nine years* after his first on 2 June 1954 – when Michael Kinane, Walter Swinburn, Philip Robinson, Cash Asmussen, Steve Cauthen, John Reid and Mick Miller had yet to draw breath.

Between The Minstrel in 1977 and Teenoso in 1983 were four losing rides.

Early in the 1978 season the big hope of Ballydoyle appeared to be Try My Best, a Northern Dancer colt unbeaten in three outings as a two-year-old which culminated in an easy victory from Sexton Blake and Camden Town in the Dewhurst Stakes. Timeform's *Racehorses* annual considered Try My Best 'practically a ready-made winner of the Two Thousand Guineas' the following year, and added that, as far as the 1978 Derby was concerned, 'we do know that Try My Best ... is built on ideal lines for the Epsom track, that his behaviour so far has been exemplary, that he is amenable to restraint, that he will therefore give himself, and be given, every chance to stay the trip, and that he will have the redoubtable assistance of Lester Piggott. So if he stays a mile and a half, he is a ready-made winner of the Derby as well.'

But Try My Best did not get to Epsom. After winning his Guineas warm-up race, the Vauxhall Trial Stakes at Phoenix Park, he started even-money favourite for the first colts' Classic, with the next runners in the betting at 14–1. Something was seriously wrong with Try My Best at Newmarket, as according to Lester 'the writing was on the wall a very long way from home, and he simply felt like a dead horse underneath me.' He finished tailed-off last. Tests indicated the onset of an infection, and for a while a slight hope was entertained that he might still run in the Derby. When this prospect was destroyed by a lacklustre home gallop, Try My Best was retired to stud (where he sired Last Tycoon, winner of the 1986 Breeders' Cup Mile).

Left looking for a Derby ride, Lester was asked by trainer Barry Hills to partner Robert Sangster's colt Hawaiian Sound, runner-up in the Chester Vase, while another decent prospect was the Ballydoyle colt Inkerman. Unraced as a two-year-old, this son of Vaguely Noble had not run at all until less than a month before the Derby. Ridden by Tommy Murphy, he won a maiden race at The Curragh on the same day that Lester landed the Irish Two Thousand Guineas for Ballydoyle on Jaazeiro. In that maiden Lester rode the runner-up Nobel Quillo, beaten four lengths, but had the ride when Inkerman returned to The Curragh to win the Gallinule Stakes and make himself a serious contender for the Derby.

In what appeared to be a very open race Lester chose to ride Inkerman, and for once he chose wrongly. About seventh or eighth at Tattenham Corner, Inkerman faded in the straight to finish out the back, while Hawaiian Sound, ridden by the great American jockey Bill Shoemaker on his first Derby ride, went very close, leading for most of the way and getting caught by the winner Shirley Heights right on the line: he was beaten a head. Lester rode Hawaiian Sound to win the Benson and Hedges Gold Cup later in the season, while Inkerman proved himself a very good horse over ten furlongs by winning the Joe McGrath Memorial Stakes at Leopardstown (now the Irish Champion Stakes), ridden by Lester. In October 1978 Inkerman was sold for $1 million – a record price for a horse in training – to continue his career with Charlie Whittingham in the USA.

The 1979 running of the Derby was the 200th in the history of the race, and events to mark the bicentenary included a special issue of stamps from the Post Office, a wide range of commemorative souvenirs and books, a facelift for the dilapidated Epsom stands and an exhibition at the Royal Academy in London – in which Lester Piggott's role in the Derby story was duly commemorated.

Of more direct interest to connections of Derby runners, the prize money added to owners' stakes for the race reached £100,000 for the first time, and the traditional speculation regarding which owner would be blessed with the assistance of L. Piggott in securing the winner's share raged through the spring. His most likely ride appeared to be Accomplice for the Sangster–O'Brien team, but eventually there emerged a booking made in heaven, and one which had the blessing of Ballydoyle on account of its special significance: in the 200th running of England's greatest Flat race, Lester would ride Milford for Her Majesty the Queen, who had won every Classic in England except the Derby.

There was a great deal to commend Milford apart from the fantasies of racing royalists. He was bred in the purple, a son of Mill Reef out of Her Majesty's 1974 One Thousand Guineas and Prix de Diane winner Highclere.

Runner-up in both his races at two, going into the Derby Milford was unbeaten in 1979, having won the White Rose Stakes at Ascot by eight lengths and the Lingfield Derby Trial by seven. He was trained by Dick Hern, who although he was yet to win a Derby had long since established himself at the peak of his profession, not least through his handling of Brigadier Gerard earlier in the 1970s and of Dunfermline, dual Classic winner for the Queen in 1977.

Dick Hern had another very strong candidate for the 1979 Derby in Troy, who had won the Classic Trial at Sandown Park and the Predominate Stakes at Goodwood, and stable jockey Willie Carson opted to ride that colt rather than Milford. The betting market responded to this decision by sending off Troy 6–1 second favourite behind 9–2 market leader Ela-Mana-Mou. Milford's starting price of 15–2 – he was joint third favourite with Two Thousand Guineas winner Tap On Wood – was more cramped than strict interpretation of his form suggested was his chance, and so it proved. Given a textbook Lester ride, Milford came round Tattenham Corner in second place, tracking Lyphard's Wish, but could find little in the straight and faded,

Lester, in the royal colours, takes Milford to the start of the 1979 Derby.

as Troy produced a memorable surge in the final furlong to win by seven lengths. Milford finished tenth. Next time out he won the Princess of Wales's Stakes at Newmarket, then ran third in the Great Voltigeur Stakes and was unplaced in the St Leger.

It was back to the old partnership with Robert Sangster and Vincent O'Brien in 1980 to ride Monteverdi, a son of Lyphard who had cost $305,000 at the Saratoga yearling sales and had won all four of his races as a juvenile, including the National Stakes at The Curragh and the Dewhurst, to make him worth, at least in the judgement of the press, $6 million. (The 'six-million dollar' tag was widely used at the time on account of the popular television programme *The Six Million-Dollar Man*.)

There was a problem about Monteverdi, however, which seriously undermined such a valuation. In the Dewhurst Stakes he had unaccountably veered violently to the left close home, a move to which Lester reacted by swiping the colt on the side of his face with his whip. Monteverdi then ran straight to the line, but a doubt persisted about his resolution, and it was by no means dispelled by his three races in 1980 before the Derby. He ran second to Nikoli at Phoenix Park, second again in the Greenham Stakes, then sported blinkers in the Irish Two Thousand Guineas, after which race Lester could not contain his exasperation, as he explained in his autobiography:

> Monteverdi simply did not try at all, and when I got off him after he'd finished fifth behind Nikoli I was so annoyed with the horse that I burst out to Vincent: 'He's useless.' I did not regret that remark. Monteverdi was one of the most unpleasant horses I ever rode, a clue to his nature being that he had very short ears. Long ears on a horse are often a sign of genuineness; the opposite interpretation can be read into short ears, and Monteverdi had the shortest of any of the O'Brien horses I rode. Furthermore, he had a mean look to him. He was, in short, a brute. But my timing of telling Vincent he was useless admittedly could have been better, as that comment was picked up by the press and published widely – not the ideal situation for Vincent, whose skill at increasing and then maintaining the value of his charges, with a view to their stallion careers, was now at a premium. That remark was the beginning of the end of my long association with Ballydoyle.

Despite his rapidly deteriorating reputation, Monteverdi started 8–1 third favourite for the Derby; Nikoli was favourite at 4–1 and Henbit, winner of the Classic Trial at Sandown Park and Chester Vase, 7–1 to give Dick Hern and Willie Carson their second successive Derby. The support for Monteverdi in the betting amply demonstrated how the magic of the O'Brien–Piggott combination could outweigh dispassionate reading of the form book, but in the race itself the colt's supporters soon had a cold dose of reality. The blinkers were left off this time, but still Monteverdi ran deplorably, finishing fourteenth behind Henbit, who cracked a cannon bone during the race and got home only on his courage – a stark contrast with the O'Brien colt.

Derby defeat, however, did not spell an especially gloomy Epsom week for Lester: he won eight races over the four days, including the Coronation Cup on Sea Chimes. His suspicion that his remark after the Irish Two Thousand Guineas was 'the beginning of the end' proved accurate. In August 1980 it was announced that Pat Eddery would ride for Ballydoyle the following year – and Lester responded by coming to an agreement to ride for Henry Cecil, who by then had been leading trainer three times.

Cecil did not have a live Derby candidate in 1981 and Lester ended up riding Shotgun, one of the two greys among his thirty-six Derby rides (the other being Bruni in 1975). Shotgun was trained at Middleham in Yorkshire by Chris Thornton and had been bred by his owner Guy Reed, whose colours were more familiar in the big handicaps with horses such as Warpath (Shotgun's sire) and Dakota than in the Derby. Shotgun had won the Heathorn Stakes at Newmarket in April before finishing runner-up in the Dante Stakes, but the Piggott factor was mainly responsible for his starting 7–1 second favourite at Epsom. Few people, however, expected the grey or any other runner to trouble the odds-on favourite Shergar – least of all Lester, who was very familiar with the Aga Khan's colt, having ridden him in both his races as a two-year-old. Shergar's position in the Derby market was due to two scintillating performances on the road to Epsom – he had won the Classic Trial at Sandown by ten lengths and the Chester Vase by twelve – and he turned the Epsom race into a procession, scooting clear early in the straight to win by ten lengths, a record margin for the Derby. (His rider Walter Swinburn was aged nineteen, after Lester the second youngest Derby-winning jockey of the twentieth century.) Shotgun never had any chance with the winner but ran on well under strong pressure to finish fourth, fourteen lengths behind Shergar. Lester's view was that Shotgun had not stayed the trip, and he subsequently reverted to shorter distances, but failed to win in three more outings. (Three and a half weeks after Epsom, Lester replaced the suspended Swinburn to ride Shergar in the Irish Derby, and won in a canter.)

The name of Lester Piggott was missing from the Derby racecard in 1982, for the first time since the problem with Bob Ward and Ione had forced him onto the sidelines twenty years earlier. His intended ride had been Simply Great, trained by Henry Cecil, but after winning the Dante Stakes the colt bruised a heel and was scratched from the Derby. It was too late for Lester to find an alternative, though he still played his part on Derby Day by offering expert comment for television viewers of the race on ITV, keeping to himself his feelings when the O'Brien–Sangster team won the big race again with Golden Fleece, ridden by Pat Eddery.

Nor was there a Cecil-trained runner in 1983. At the beginning of the season there had been a very lively Warren Place hope in Dunbeath, who as a two-year-old had won the Royal Lodge Stakes and William Hill Futurity (as the Observer Gold Cup had become) at Doncaster so impressively that he had been bought by Sheikh Mohammed for a reported £6 million in November 1982. Despite being beaten in the Heathorn Stakes at Newmarket, Dunbeath vied for Derby favouritism with Dick Hern-trained Gorytus, a son of Nijinsky out of the One Thousand Guineas winner Glad Rags who had been a brilliant two-year-old until flopping when very hot favourite for the Dewhurst Stakes, arousing fears that he had been doped. But Dunbeath could finish only a distant third behind Hot Touch when odds-on in the Dante Stakes and was ruled out of Epsom.

With Dunbeath out of the picture, Lester was approached about riding the French-trained Esprit du Nord, then about the Irish Two Thousand Guineas winner Wassl, and then about Tolomeo, runner-up to Lomond in the Two Thousand Guineas when ridden by Gianfranco Dettori. While mulling over that last possibility he was asked by trainer Geoffrey Wragg to consider his runner, Teenoso. Suspecting that Tolomeo would not stay, Lester rode Teenoso in a gallop at Newmarket two weeks before the race, and was so impressed with the feeling the colt gave him that he agreed to take the ride.

Geoff Wragg's father Harry Wragg has a unique place in Derby history as the only person to have both ridden and trained Derby winners. Nicknamed 'The Head Waiter' on account of his exquisite tactical skills in the saddle, he rode the winner three times and trained 66–1 outsider Psidium – turned down by Lester – to land the big race in 1961. Harry Wragg retired from training at the end of the 1982 season, so Geoff – who had been his father's assistant for nearly thirty years – was in his first season training in 1983.

The principal patron of the Wragg yard, Abington Place on Newmarket's Bury Road, was Hong Kong-based shipping and insurance broker Eric Moller, whose racing operation, founded with his late brother Ralph (popularly known as 'Budgie'), was based at the White Lodge Stud. The brothers had founded the stud in 1944, and over four decades their distinctive colours – chocolate, gold braid and sleeves, quartered cap – had become a familiar sight on British racecourses through the achievements of a succession of top class horses including Lacquer, Sovereign, Full Dress II, Moulton (unplaced in Roberto's Derby but winner of the 1973 Benson and Hedges Gold Cup), Freefoot, Cherry Hinton and Amaranda. They had bred Teenoso by sending their mare Furioso – runner-up to Polygamy in the 1974 Oaks – to Kentucky to be mated with Nelson Bunker Hunt's 1976 Prix du Jockey-Club winner Youth. Sadly, Budgie Moller died early in 1980 and never saw the foal produced by that mating, born in April that year.

Teenoso's two-year-old career produced nothing to pick him out as a future Derby winner. He only once finished in the money in three races, picking up £262 for coming fourth in a maiden at Newmarket on his third outing in October 1982. (One of the horses behind him that day was Amrullah, who in later years would become fabled as the horse who refused to win.) Timeform's *Racehorses of 1982* rated Diesis the season's top two-year-old on 133 and had Teenoso on 86 – though, to be fair, noted that the Moller colt 'has plenty of scope and promises to make up into a useful three-year-old'.

The level of understatement which that remark represented was not immediately apparent in spring 1983. Teenoso made his three-year-old debut in a maiden race over ten and a half furlongs at Haydock Park in April and was beaten a neck by Welsh Idol. That was encouraging enough to make him favourite for his next race, the April Maiden Stakes over a mile and a half at Newmarket, and here he registered his first win in tremendous style: ridden by Steve Cauthen, he took up the running with over a quarter of a

mile to go and won unchallenged by eight lengths, beating eighteen rivals. Next came a major step up in class in the Lingfield Derby Trial in early May. The Michael Stoute-trained grey Shearwalk, who had beaten Dunbeath in the Heathorn Stakes, started favourite, but Teenoso, again ridden by Steve Cauthen, revelled in the heavy going that day to win by three lengths. Steve Cauthen would be required to ride The Noble Player in the Derby for his retainer Robert Sangster: hence Geoff Wragg's call to Lester.

Two things about Teenoso were now clear: that he was a stayer, and that he could act extremely well on soft ground. Both were key factors as far as the Derby was concerned.

The spring of 1983 was exceptionally wet, and all around the country racecourses were affected by waterlogging. Of the eighty-one meetings scheduled before the York May Meeting, no fewer than twenty-six were called off because of the conditions, including the whole of the Chester May Meeting, where Teenoso had been due to run in the Chester Vase. The prevailing ground played havoc with preparation of Derby candidates, and with the form lines looking so confusing and running plans impossible to confirm, an abnormally large proportion of the original entries remained in the Derby. At one point there was a distinct possibility that Jockey Club handicappers would be drafted in to whittle the potential field down to the safety maximum for the course and distance, thirty-three runners.

As it turned out, such intervention was not necessary. Twenty-three runners were declared (though Gorytus, who had been an intended starter, was not among them on account of the very soft going) and it looked an open race – if indeed the race were to take place at all. After fierce thunderstorms and a torrential downpour throughout the night before, there was a real possibility that the Derby would be abandoned for the first time in its history. The Epsom stewards inspected the course at dawn on Derby Day to judge whether it was fit for racing. It was – but the official going for the race was declared 'heavy' for the first time in over half a century. Of the twenty-three horses declared overnight as definite runners, two were withdrawn because of the ground, leaving twenty-one to go to post.

By now the idea that Lester Piggott was the 'Housewives' Choice' for every Derby – the term was derived from the music programme broadcast each weekday morning on the radio, ostensibly to lift the spirits of housewives as they went about their daily chores – had become a well-worn cliché of racing journalism, and was wheeled out annually. 'Lester's the man the housewives put their money on', declared Coral Bookmakers' representative George Irvine to one newspaper, while another made a link with the general election campaign then in full swing with 'WIVES VOTE FOR LESTER! – HE'S DERBY DELIGHT'.

The 1983 general election, in which the country was asked to choose between a second term of Margaret Thatcher and a Labour government led by Michael Foot, was taking place eight days after the Derby, and provided comic business in the big-race prognostications of comedian Eric Morecambe in the *Daily Express*: 'In a recent opinion poll, Lester Piggott came out top as the person most people would like to see at No. 10. It's what is known as a gallop poll.' Asked whether Lester could win the Derby for the ninth time, Morecambe replied: 'It's all according to whether he's taken his Epsom salts. They make him go round the bend faster, y'know.'

When the serious business of on-course betting commenced, Teenoso opened at 3–1 favourite, then drifted right out to 6–1 before late money brought him in to 9–2 favourite at the off. Salmon Leap – owned by Robert Sangster, trained by Vincent O'Brien and ridden by Pat Eddery, and winner of the Nijinsky Stakes at Leopardstown – started second favourite at 11–2. Dick Hern-trained Morcon, winner of the Predominate Stakes, was on 17–2, with Two Thousand Guineas winner Lomond apparently the Ballydoyle second string at 9–1. Wassl started at 10–1, with Tolomeo bracketed on 14–1 with another Irish challenger Carlingford Castle, winner of the Ballysax Stakes and Gallinule Stakes at The Curragh: his jockey Michael Kinane was having his first ride in the Derby, and wore not Flat racing silks but his owner's woollen jumping colours, which she thought would bring her luck. Pluralisme, the only French challenger, started at 18–1 with Shearwalk, and Slewpy, a rare Derby raider from the USA, was virtually unsupported on 100–1.

* * *

After Geoff Wragg had approached me about riding Teenoso at Epsom I arranged to ride work on the horse at Newmarket, about two weeks before the Derby. I liked the feel he gave me, and in a very open year he seemed to have a lot going for him as a Derby candidate. Both his breeding and his form showed that he would certainly stay, he would go on the likely ground, and though he was quite a big horse he had a very relaxed style of galloping. They always go fast in the Derby, and a tearaway is bound to use up his energy too soon, so it is important to have a horse who will go well within himself until asked to step up the tempo. A week before the Derby I rode Teenoso in quite a serious gallop and remained very pleased with him. There was nothing in the race that year I'd rather have been on.

It was very unusual to ride a Derby on really heavy ground, and there's not often much give at Epsom, so Teenoso was a case of having exactly the right horse for unusual conditions – the right horse at the right time.

Knowing that stamina was his forte, I had him out of the starting stalls quickly, and got him to settle in about third place. He had no trouble acting on the heavy ground or on the course, and by the top of the hill I could sense that there were plenty of other runners ill at ease with both. Going down to Tattenham Corner we were still travelling easily in third, one horse off the rails, behind the outsiders Mitilini and Tivian, with Neorion just outside me. At this point Teenoso was going so easily that I was able to take a look over my right shoulder to see if anything was likely to come from off the pace – always a difficult proposition in such heavy going – and was reassured by what I saw. They were pretty well all flat to the boards.

Once we straightened up I knew there was no point in hanging around. Teenoso would stay all day and would gallop all the way to the line, so I just let him go and set sail for home. He was soon three

Tattenham Corner, 1983. Mitilini (Geoff Baxter) leads, as Lester takes a good look at Brian Rouse on Neorion. Tivian (Sandy Barclay) is on the rails behind the leader.

lengths up, and though Guns Of Navarone made a spirited attempt to close the gap he couldn't keep it up, and Carlingford Castle went past him into second. But Teenoso was always going easily, and he galloped on without my ever feeling for a second that he wouldn't last home. At the line he was three lengths clear of Carlingford Castle, with Shearwalk another three lengths further behind in third, just beating Salmon Leap. I learned later that both Carlingford Castle and Shearwalk had encountered difficulty getting a clear run, though this didn't make the slightest difference to the result, and that Yawa, ridden by Philip Waldron, had clipped the heels of Shearwalk on the run downhill and fallen. Apparently Gianfranco Dettori had caused all sorts of problems when cutting across to the rails on Tolomeo as we came down the hill. As I've often said: if you lay up handy in the Derby you're less likely to suffer interference from argy-bargy coming down the hill.

Teenoso might not have been my classiest Derby winner, but he was certainly my easiest.

*　*　*

While the housewives of Britain beat a path to the betting shops to collect their winnings, the press dusted off the by now well-worn superlatives, and the headline writers were in ninth heaven with such offerings as 'PIGGOTT ON CLOUD NINE!' … 'LESTER DRESSES UP TO THE NINES ON TEENOSO' … 'KING LESTER THE NINTH'.

Most papers quoted Lester's characteristically phlegmatic summing up of the race that 'All I had to do was let him go and it was all over', but their own reports were less dismissive of the level of jockeyship involved.

For Peter Scott in the *Daily Telegraph*, Teenoso's victory was 'a performance of ruthless efficiency', and for Jim Stanford in the *Daily Mail* it 'set the seal on probably the greatest career in racing history.' In *The Times*, Michael Phillips wrote that 'Everyone loves occasions like these – a big winner ridden by Piggott – everyone, I should say, except the bookmakers, who were left counting their costs on this occasion, because on Derby Day people tend to follow Piggott blind. Yesterday backers of the winning combination can never have felt at all uneasy.'

Opposite:
The 1983 finish: Lester and Teenoso cruise in from Carlingford Castle (Michael Kinane). Shearwalk (third) is out of the picture, with Salmon Leap (Pat Eddery, light cap) fourth and Guns Of Navarone (Philip Robinson) fifth.

The *Daily Star* described how 'The man who could handle the tricky Epsom switchback course in his sleep gave his fellow jockeys a familiar view on favourite Teenoso yesterday – his famous backside', while much later, in its *Racehorses of 1983* annual, Timeform was able to give a more reflective view of Lester: 'He seems somehow to grow neither older nor less effective as the years go by – Teenoso was his thirtieth ride in the Derby – and his mastery of the Derby course in particular is complete. His great strength, demonstrated so effectively on Roberto and The Minstrel at Epsom, wasn't called into play in 1983 but his handling of Teenoso was an object lesson in how to ride a proven stayer in the Derby.'

Eric Moller, aged seventy-six when Teenoso won, revealed that he had not had a penny on his colt, and then told the press: 'Don't forget I rode the winner of the Shanghai National in 1941, and my father rode a winner in China in 1896!'

The time of the race confirmed the nature of the conditions. It took Teenoso 2 minutes 49.07 seconds to win the Derby, making the 1983 renewal the slowest since Common took 2 minutes 56.8 seconds in 1891, a race run on ground saturated by torrential rain.

The twenty-nine years between Lester's first Derby winner and his last is the longest period between a jockey's winners in modern Derby history, but not the longest in the whole history of the race. Frank Buckle won his first on John Bull in 1792 – the thirteenth running – and his fifth and last on Emilius in 1823, a gap of thirty-one years. Nor was Lester, forty-seven years old when winning on Teenoso, by any means the oldest Derby-winning jockey, even in recent history. Scobie Breasley was fifty-two when winning on Charlottown in 1966 and Charlie Smirke fifty-one when winning on Hard Ridden in 1958, as was Rae Johnstone when winning on Lavandin in 1956. The oldest Derby-winning jockey of all was J. Forth, reported to be over sixty when winning on Frederick in 1829.

The day after Teenoso's victory Lester rode Be My Native to win the Coronation Cup, bringing his tally in that historic race to … nine.

* * *

Despite the ground conditions, Teenoso did not have a particularly hard race in the Derby and was trained for the Irish Derby three and

a half weeks later. This time the going was good to firm, and he did not reproduce his Epsom form, finishing third behind Shareef Dancer and Caerleon, the colt owned by Robert Sangster and trained by Vincent who had won the Prix du Jockey-Club. This seemed to show up Teenoso as a below-average Derby winner, and his reputation was not enhanced next time out, when he could finish only third to Seymour Hicks in the Great Voltigeur Stakes. It transpired that he had sustained a leg injury in this race, which ruled him out of the St Leger – in which he must have had a wonderful chance, given his reserves of stamina – and saw him retired for the season.

Kept in training as a four-year-old, he opened his 1984 campaign by running third behind Gay Lemur and Dazari in the John Porter Stakes at Newbury in April. He then won the Ormonde Stakes at Chester – Pat Eddery rode him on that occasion as I was suspended – and went to France for his first major target of the season, the Grand Prix de Saint-Cloud. Here his wellbeing and ebullience got the better of him – or rather of me. As we turned to go to the start at the end of the pre-race parade he was so keen to get on with matters that he threw his head back just as I was leaning forward to canter him down, giving me an almighty clout in the face. I was quite badly cut above and below my right eye, but decided to go ahead and ride in the race – which is just as well, as Teenoso turned in a marvellously brave performance on ground firmer than he liked and won narrowly from Fly Me, with Esprit du Nord third. I had been treated with sticking plasters, but the cuts had reopened during the race and I returned to the winner's enclosure with blood all over my colours.

Teenoso then went to Ascot for the King George VI and Queen Elizabeth Diamond Stakes. This is always a very high-class event, but the 1984 running was exceptionally high-quality even by the standards of the race. The five-year-old mare Time Charter, winner of the 1982 Oaks and 1983 King George, was favourite, having most recently won the Coronation Cup; Darshaan had won the Prix du Jockey-Club from the Irish Two Thousand Guineas winner Sadler's Wells, who reopposed him here, having in the meantime beaten Time Charter in the Eclipse Stakes; Dahar had won the Prix Lupin; Sun

Princess had won the Oaks and St Leger the previous year; Tolomeo, whom I could have ridden in Teenoso's Derby, had won the Arlington Million in Chicago later in 1983; the filly Luth Enchantée had won the Prix Jacques le Marois and Prix du Moulin in 1983 and run fourth behind Teenoso at Saint-Cloud.

I knew that if I could make his stamina come into play Teenoso would have a first-rate chance, even against such opponents – he was only third favourite – and on going which was officially given as good to firm. As soon as the stalls opened I shot him into the lead, and though Sun Princess's hard-ridden pacemaker His Honour took over after about half a mile, Teenoso led again when that horse weakened five furlongs out. We came into the short Ascot straight half a length to the good, and I kept pushing him out as the others came to challenge. Only Sadler's Wells could make much impression, and he ran on gamely to try and catch us. He came within a length or so, but Teenoso showed his true mettle and just kept going. A hundred and fifty yards out Sadler's Wells cracked, and we stayed on to win by two and a half lengths. A superb performance.

The King George victory made Teenoso favourite for the Prix de l'Arc de Triomphe, and I really would have fancied his chances at Longchamp – especially on the soft ground on which the Arc is so often run. But with just a couple of days to go before the race he was found to have heat in his off-foreleg, a sign of tendon strain. The Arc was out of the question, and he was retired to stud.

Some people seem to have forgotten just how good a horse Teenoso was. Maybe the 1983 running was not the best Derby ever – of the beaten horses, only Tolomeo showed top-class form later when winning the 1983 Arlington Million – but Teenoso could do no more than win it very easily. And in the 1984 King George he took on one of the very best fields ever assembled for that race and beat them fair and square. That day he was a true champion.

*   *   *

One of only two Derby winners ever to win the King George as a four-year-old (the other was Royal Palace in 1968), Teenoso stood as a stallion

Following pages:
The winner's circle.

initially at the Highclere Stud in Berkshire, where he replaced 1979 Derby winner Troy, who had died in 1983 at the tragically early age of seven. He was moved from there to stand, principally as a National Hunt stallion, at Shade Oak Stud in Shropshire and then at Pitts Farm Stud in Dorset, where he died in October 1999 at the age of nineteen. His offspring include Sir Peter Lely, fourth in the 1996 Grand National, and Young Spartacus, winner of the Racing Post Chase in 2001.

For the final word on Lester's ninth Derby win we can do no better than quote from Tony Morris's column in the *Sporting Life*, published two days after Teenoso's victory:

> It has been my inestimable privilege to witness – for two decades – the supreme artist plying his craft from the saddle, his genius as sublime as that of a Rembrandt or a Beethoven, and his accomplishments on the same plane. In the sporting world there has been nobody to match him in his lifetime … George Best bestrode his sphere like a Colossus for a season, Gary Sobers his for perhaps five, but for the best part of three decades – truly the best part of us who know – Lester has been the pre-eminent leader of his field. No, I don't need you to tell me that plenty of other jockeys would probably have won on Teenoso – and on one or two of his other Derby winners as well. He said himself it was easy, and you had to believe him, the way the race was won. But wasn't it a superb example of the master at work, doing everything right, executing every manoeuvre to the perfect standard he has set? And didn't Wednesday provide a ray of light in a period of general gloom and despondency, an affirmation of traditional values, with the essential rightness of it all? Suddenly you could sense that God's in his heaven, Lester's won the Derby, and all's right with the world!

Teenoso

Pedigree

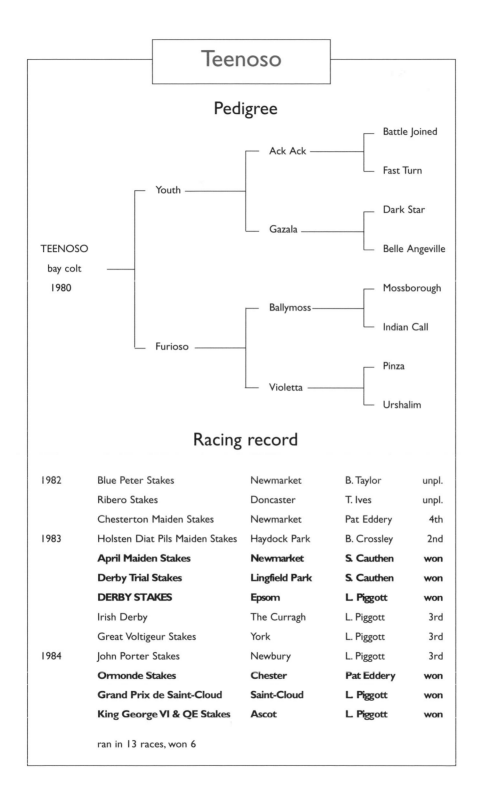

TEENOSO
bay colt
1980

- Youth
  - Ack Ack
    - Battle Joined
    - Fast Turn
  - Gazala
    - Dark Star
    - Belle Angeville
- Furioso
  - Ballymoss
    - Mossborough
    - Indian Call
  - Violetta
    - Pinza
    - Urshalim

Racing record

1982	Blue Peter Stakes	Newmarket	B. Taylor	unpl.
	Ribero Stakes	Doncaster	T. Ives	unpl.
	Chesterton Maiden Stakes	Newmarket	Pat Eddery	4th
1983	Holsten Diat Pils Maiden Stakes	Haydock Park	B. Crossley	2nd
	April Maiden Stakes	**Newmarket**	**S. Cauthen**	**won**
	Derby Trial Stakes	**Lingfield Park**	**S. Cauthen**	**won**
	DERBY STAKES	**Epsom**	**L. Piggott**	**won**
	Irish Derby	The Curragh	L. Piggott	3rd
	Great Voltigeur Stakes	York	L. Piggott	3rd
1984	John Porter Stakes	Newbury	L. Piggott	3rd
	Ormonde Stakes	**Chester**	**Pat Eddery**	**won**
	Grand Prix de Saint-Cloud	**Saint-Cloud**	**L. Piggott**	**won**
	King George VI & QE Stakes	**Ascot**	**L. Piggott**	**won**

ran in 13 races, won 6

THE FINAL RIDES

Previous pages:
*Going to the start of his
thirty-sixth and final
Derby ride on
Khamaseen, 1994.*

Lester started the 1984 season still stable jockey to Henry Cecil, though his position was looking in jeopardy on account of a rift with the Paris-based art dealer Daniel Wildenstein, one of Cecil's principal owners. First there had been a brouhaha over his riding of Wildenstein's two-year-old colt Vacarme in the Richmond Stakes at Goodwood in July 1983. Vacarme won but was disqualified and placed last after Lester had squeezed through a gap on the rail to incur the displeasure not only of the Goodwood stewards – he received a stiff suspension for careless riding – but also of the colt's owner. Then he was asked by French trained Patrick-Louis Biancone to ride Wildenstein's filly All Along in the Prix de l'Arc de Triomphe, and when it turned out that he would be riding Awaasif for trainer John Dunlop the French camp took severe umbrage. Lester protested that it was all an innocent mix-up, but Wildenstein declared that 'Piggott will never ride for me again' – and that included his horses trained by Henry Cecil.

So Cecil's principal hope for the 1984 Derby, the Wildenstein-owned Claude Monet, was not an option for Lester. The colt would be ridden by Steve Cauthen, and rumours were rife that Cauthen would soon be taking over from Lester at Warren Place. On the Sunday morning that these rumours went into black and white in the newspapers, Lester was phoned by trainer Guy Harwood and offered a very live Derby ride: Prince Khalid Abdullah's colt Alphabatim, who had won the William Hill Futurity as a two-year-old and the Classic Trial at Sandown Park and Lingfield Derby Trial (the latter by six lengths) already in 1984.

Greville Starkey, Alphabatim's usual jockey, was out of action following a bad fall, and Lester accepted the offer.

Alphabatim started second favourite at Epsom at 11–2. The market leader came from the Sangster–O'Brien–Eddery camp in El Gran Senor, whose Derby starting price of 8–11 was a fair reflection of his chance, judging from the way he had overpowered Chief Singer and Lear Fan to win the Two Thousand Guineas. Claude Monet was joint third favourite at 12–1.

It proved impossible for Lester to ride his usual Derby race on Alphabatim, who did not have the pace to lay up with the leaders. At Tattenham Corner he was nearer last than first, and though he made steady progress up the straight he could only finish fifth, a short head and six lengths behind the winner Secreto, trained by Vincent O'Brien's son David. The short head by which

Secreto beat El Gran Senor supposedly wiped millions off the value of the Ballydoyle colt and triggered a major talking point. Had Pat Eddery taken things too easily on the favourite? But Lester is adamant that, contrary to legend, he did not mutter 'Missing me?' to the shell-shocked Robert Sangster and Vincent O'Brien as he walked past them on the way to the weighing room.

Alphabatim went on to run third in the St Leger behind Commanche Run (Lester's record-breaking twenty-eighth Classic win). The remainder of his races in 1984 were in the USA, where he won the Hollywood Turf Cup International, and he continued his career there, trained in California by John Gosden.

That the 1985 season would be Lester's last was an open secret long before he himself announced it formally, and he had been replaced as Henry Cecil's stable jockey by Steve Cauthen and was again operating as a freelance. So in the circumstances the Derby of 1985 took on a special significance: which horse would provide Lester Piggott's final Derby ride?

The answer was Theatrical, trained in Ireland by Dermot Weld. Winner of his only race as a two-year-old, Theatrical had run twice in 1985 before the Derby, winning the Ballysax Stakes at The Curragh and then the Derrinstown Stud Derby Trial at Leopardstown, and seemed to have a decent chance at Epsom: he started at 10–1. Only the 9–4 favourite Slip Anchor (ten-length winner of the Lingfield Derby Trial, trained by Henry Cecil and ridden by Steve Cauthen), Shadeed (winner of the Two Thousand Guineas when ridden by Lester) and Vincent O'Brien-trained Law Society, winner of the Chester Vase, started at shorter odds. Slip Anchor led from the start, and Theatrical, though handy enough at Tattenham Corner, could never get in a blow. Nor could any other runner, and Slip Anchor – who would have been Lester's mount had he not left Warren Place – won easily by seven lengths from Law Society. Theatrical finished seventh, beaten about twenty-five lengths.

After Epsom, Theatrical was runner-up to Law Society in the Irish Derby (Lester rode the third, Damister), ran unplaced in the Phoenix Champion Stakes (Lester rode the winner Commanche Run), and then provided Lester with his first Breeders' Cup ride when unplaced behind Pebbles in the 1985 Breeders' Cup Turf at Aqueduct racetrack, New York. He failed to win in six outings in England, Germany and the USA in 1986, though was beaten only a neck by Manila in the Breeders' Cup Turf at Santa Anita in 1986, with the European champion Dancing Brave well behind in fourth. By then he was trained in the USA by Bobby Frankel, but was subsequently sold to Allen

Paulson (later owner of Arazi and Cigar), who sent him to trainer Bill Mott. Theatrical ran in his third consecutive Breeders' Cup Turf at Hollywood Park in 1987 and this time he won, beating Arc winner Trempolino after a tremendous battle up the home stretch. Having also won several other big American races in 1987, including the Turf Classic and Man o' War Stakes, he was named Champion Turf Male for that year in the Eclipse Awards. Theatrical retired winner of seven of his fourteen starts and nearly $3 million in prize money. Lester's thirty-second and final Derby ride, though well beaten at Epsom, got better as he got older, and matured into an extremely good horse.

Except, of course, that Theatrical was not Lester's final Derby ride. The events which saw him retire from the saddle in October 1985, hold a trainer's licence for the best part of two seasons, spend one year and one day in prison after conviction for tax fraud before being released on parole, and then make a sensational return to race-riding in October 1990 are sufficiently well documented not to need repeating here. But in spring 1991 this extraordinary sequence of events led to the revival of the great British tradition of asking: 'What will Lester ride in the Derby?'

The answer for 1991 was Hokusai, owned by Lester's old friend Charles St George (owner of Bruni) and trained by Henry Cecil – only Lester's second Derby ride for the trainer, after Arthurian back in 1974. Hokusai was unbeaten in two races as a two-year-old, and started his three-year-old season with a good third to Marju in the Craven Stakes at Newmarket. Lester rode the colt in that race, but was on Bog Trotter, trained by his son-in-law William Haggas, in the Two Thousand Guineas. Michael Kinane took the ride on Hokusai, who finished eighth behind Mystiko; Bog Trotter came twelfth. Cash Asmussen rode Hokusai when the colt ran fourth in the Prix Jean Prat at Longchamp ten days before the Derby, and not long after that St George asked Lester to take the ride at Epsom.

Hokusai was sent off at 25–1 for the Derby, and in a small field of only thirteen runners was kept handy through the early stages. At Tattenham Corner he was about fifth as Mystiko led into the straight, but had no answer when Generous blazed into the lead and ran on to win by five lengths from Marju. Hokusai finished seventh, but the Piggott family could claim some credit for the result: Alan Munro, rider of Generous, had prepared for his ride by watching videos of Lester's nine victories, and talking through them with Lester's father Keith.

After the Derby, Lester rode Hokusai into third in the St James's Palace Stakes at Royal Ascot, beaten just over two lengths by Marju, but top American jockey Chris McCarron was in the saddle when the colt finished fifth in the Del Mar International Derby in California in August.

In contrast with the 25–1 shot Hokusai, Lester's Derby ride in 1992 was thought to have a major chance and went off 13–2 favourite. Rodrigo de Triano – a son of El Gran Senor named after the lookout on the ship in which Christopher Columbus had discovered the New World 500 years earlier – was owned by Lester's old comrade-in-arms Robert Sangster and trained at Manton in Wiltshire by Peter Chapple-Hyam, Sangster's stepson-in-law and a young trainer in only his second season with a licence. Rodrigo de Triano had won the Champagne Stakes and Middle Park Stakes as a two-year-old, and after Willie Carson had ridden him to finish fourth in the Greenham Stakes, Sangster asked Lester to ride the colt in the Two Thousand Guineas: Carson would be claimed for that race by his retainer Hamdan al Maktoum.

Rodrigo de Triano won the Two Thousand Guineas by a length and a half from Lucky Lindy, giving Lester his thirtieth Classic in England at the age of fifty-

The first Derby of Lester's Second Coming, 1991. The grey Mystiko (Michael Roberts) leads from another grey Arokat (Paul Eddery) and the winner Generous (Alan Munro), with Lester (white cap) and Hokusai on the rails behind the leader.

six, and then won the Irish Two Thousand Guineas by a length from Ezzoud.

The prospect of a tenth Piggott victory in the Derby seemed a very real one, though there were doubts about the colt's ability to last the mile and a half, and about how he would act on the course. Events proved that such doubts were justified. Never in the hunt once the heat was turned on from the top of the hill, he finished ninth of the eighteen runners behind his stable companion Dr Devious, a performance which Lester felt needed an explanation: 'I came in for some criticism afterwards from people who said I never put him in the race with any chance, but the fact was that he simply did not act on the track at all, and I was not prepared to risk ruining him for the future by subjecting him to too hard a contest at Epsom.' The wisdom of that judgement was underlined later in the season, when Lester rode Rodrigo de Triano to win the Juddmonte International Stakes at York (previously the Benson and Hedges Gold Cup) and the Champion Stakes. After finishing last in the Breeders' Cup Mile at Gulfstream Park, Florida, when ridden by Walter Swinburn — Lester was in the emergency room after a crashing fall from the sprinter Mr Brooks earlier in the afternoon — Rodrigo de Triano was retired to stud in Japan.

Another old friend supplied Lester's ride in the 1993 Derby — Vincent O'Brien. Fatherland, a son of Sadler's Wells, had won four of his five races as a two-year-old, including the prestigious National Stakes at The Curragh. In spring 1993 he came second to Massyar in the Two Thousand Guineas

Trial at Leopardstown (ridden by Lester and beaten two lengths) and filled the same spot in the Irish Two Thousand Guineas, failing only by a head to catch Barathea after Lester had conjured a flying finish out of him. Lester's autobiography takes up the story:

> The result at the Curragh opened up an intriguing possibility for the 1993 Derby. Fatherland was trained by Vincent O'Brien and ran in the colours of his wife Jacqueline, and on the form of the Irish Two Thousand Guineas would go to Epsom with a real chance, though on the evidence of the race it was impossible to know whether he would stay the Derby distance or not. Fatherland always tended to hang to the left a little so we thought that Epsom might suit him, and we were not alone. His price at the off was 8–1, third market choice behind odds-on Tenby – an unbeaten colt who had won the Newmarket Stakes and Dante Stakes en route to Epsom – and his stable companion Commander In Chief. The latter won well under Mick Kinane while Fatherland, whom I had moved up early in the straight to try to get into a challenging position, simply failed to stay. To have won my tenth Derby on a horse trained by Vincent, whose retirement was certain to come in the foreseeable future, would have been a fairy tale even by my standards, but it was not to be. Fatherland ran only once more in Europe – fourth in the Prix Eugene Adam at Saint-Cloud – before being moved to the USA, where he sadly had to be destroyed after breaking a pastern in the Hollywood Derby.

Fatherland was Lester's ninth Derby ride on a horse trained by Vincent O'Brien – a quarter of his rides in the race came from Ballydoyle – and the association had yielded four winners: Sir Ivor, Nijinsky, Roberto and The Minstrel. O'Brien trained six Derby winners in all – Larkspur and Golden Fleece in addition to Lester's four – and remains the most successful Derby trainer of the post-war period. He retired in 1994.

Lester's thirty-sixth and final Derby ride in 1994 – and this time it was indeed final – was Khamaseen, owned by Prince Faisal and trained at Arundel by John Dunlop. This colt by Slip Anchor had shown some ability as a two-year-old – his best form was to finish fourth to King's Theatre in the Racing Post Trophy at Doncaster – and won his first race as a three-year-old by beating a solitary opponent at Nottingham. He was then runner-up to Linney Head in the Classic Trial at Sandown Park. Khamaseen and his fifty-eight-year-old jockey

Following pages: Lester at Epsom Downs for the opening of the Piggott Gates, painted by Roy Miller, in June 1996. The horse numbered 25 is his 1983 Derby winner Teenoso.

1981 OAKS
BLUE WIND

started at 33–1 for the Derby and ran very well to finish just out of the money in fifth place behind the favourite Erhaab: having come into the straight in second place, Khamaseen could not quicken in the final quarter of a mile, but had run honourably in defeat. He was then well beaten in the Irish Derby and in the Gordon Stakes at Goodwood. Kept in training in 1995 Khamaseen won a small race at Nottingham and the Coppa d'Oro di Milano, but his best effort was to finish third to Double Trigger in the Goodwood Cup.

By then Lester had retired – for good.

The name 'L. PIGGOTT' would no longer appear on the number board before the Derby, but Lester still had a couple of footnotes to contribute to the history of the world's greatest Flat race.

Four days before the 1996 running the Epsom executive staged the formal opening of the Piggott Gates, through which the Derby runners would leave the parade ring on their way out to the course. (The layout had been altered since Lester's riding day, so that the parade ring was now behind the grandstand, rather than down the course beyond the winning post.) These gates display portraits by artist Roy Miller of the nine Derby winners, along with other famous horses – such as the great filly Petite Etoile – partnered by Lester at Epsom.

That was not the only Piggott input into the 1996 Derby. Lester's son-in-law William Haggas trained a live candidate in Shaamit, who had won one of his two races as a two-year-old. Haggas had been unable to get a prep race into the colt on account of a series of setbacks, and asked Lester to try the horse out on the home gallops before they decided whether it was worth going for the Derby: 'My nine Derby winners had shown me that the quality a horse most needs for the race is balance,' Lester wrote, 'and after that gallop I assured William that Shaamit, clearly a colt of great quality, would not fail on that score. He'd got what it takes, and had to have a go.' When Shaamit swooped late under Michael Hills to beat Dushyantor, Lester related: 'It was a great family triumph, and to have played a part, however small, in Shaamit's preparation was a huge thrill. It really felt like my tenth Derby winner.'

*   *   *

Lester's Derbys spanned forty-three years and took in thirty-six rides, his first winner separated from his last by twenty-nine years. He rode the winner nine times – three more than any other jockey in history – and the runner-up four times, and year after year displayed a complete mastery of riding in what many of his contemporaries considered the most difficult contest in world racing.

How does he rate the nine winners?

A distinction has to be made between the overall brilliance of the horse through his career, or in another race, and how that horse was on Derby Day. For me Nijinsky felt at his peak when winning the King George at Ascot, and that day gave me the best feel of any middle-distance horse I ever rode. But in the Derby itself the performance of Sir Ivor was more exhilarating than Nijinsky's, so I have to rank him my best Derby winner, with Nijinsky second. Third place would go to Crepello, a brilliant horse in the Two Thousand Guineas and the Derby, but sadly denied the opportunity ever to race against older horses and prove his true greatness.

The Minstrel had the perfect Derby physique, and I never rode a horse in the race with a more courageous attitude. Roberto was very good when conditions suited – witness his beating Brigadier Gerard – but fallible when they did not. Teenoso and St Paddy both slaughtered the opposition in the Derby and both have both been underrated since. Teenoso beat a fantastic King George field fair and square, while St Paddy did not help himself by pulling so hard, but off a fast pace was in the very top class. Never Say Die is so long ago that it's hard for me to recall just how good he was, but he won the Derby very easily, and only a top-class horse could win the St Leger by twelve lengths. I suppose that Empery has to be judged the worst of the nine: although he won well enough at Epsom, the overall level of his form left him well behind the other eight.

But as I said earlier, on the day each of them felt like a true champion. The Derby winner always does.

FACTS AND FIGURES

Previous pages:
Another Derby for Lester
– winning the German
variety at Hamburg in
1957 on Orsini.

Lester's Derbys, 1951–1994

The Complete List

Below are listed all thirty-six rides Lester Piggott had in the Derby between 1951 and 1994, with the horse's trainer, starting price, finishing position ('unplaced' if out of first six), the official form book's description of each horse's running – with the *Raceform* shorthand expanded a little for ease of reading – and the number of runners that year. (Grateful thanks to Raceform for permission to reproduce the form book comments.)

1951
ZUCCHERO
(trained by Ken Cundell)
28–1
unplaced behind Arctic Prince
hood [i.e. Zucchero wore blinkers]: left start
33 ran

1952
GAY TIME
(Noel Cannon)
100–7
second to Tulyar, beaten ¾ length
headway straight: challenged distance: hung left: no extra near finish
33 ran

1953
PRINCE CHARLEMAGNE
66–1
unplaced behind Pinza
[no comment in *Raceform*]
27 ran

1954
NEVER SAY DIE
(Joe Lawson)
33–1
won by 2 lengths from Arabian Night
5th straight: led 2 furlongs out: soon clear
22 ran

1955
WINDSOR SUN
(Seamus McGrath)
33–1
unplaced behind Phil Drake
prominent 6 furlongs
23 ran

1956
AFFILIATION ORDER
(Charles Jerdein)
33–1
unplaced behind Lavandin
11th straight: no headway
27 ran

1957

CREPELLO

(Noel Murless)

6–4 favourite

won by 1½ lengths from Ballymoss

looked well: 6th straight: led over 1 furlong

out: quickened close home

22 ran

1958

BOCCACCIO

(Noel Murless)

20–1

unplaced behind Hard Ridden

sweating: hood: 5th straight: failed to run on

20 ran

1959

CARNOUSTIE

(Noel Murless)

10–1

6th behind Parthia

8th straight: no headway final 2 furlongs

20 ran

1960

ST PADDY

(Noel Murless)

7–1

won by 3 lengths from Alcaeus

looked well: 4th straight: led over 2 furlongs

out: quickened inside final furlong: ran on

17 ran

1961

no ride

1962

no ride

1963

CORPORA

(Ernie Fellows)

100–8

5th behind Relko

hood: 4th straight: no headway final 3 furlongs

26 ran

1964

SWEET MOSS

(Noel Murless)

100–8

unplaced behind Santa Claus

8th straight: never reach leaders

17 ran

1965

MEADOW COURT

(Paddy Prendergast)

10–1

second to Sea Bird II, beaten 2 lengths

prominent 7 furlongs: 3rd straight: good

headway final furlong: ran on

22 ran

1966

RIGHT NOBLE

(Vincent O'Brien)

9–2 joint favourite (with Pretendre)

unplaced behind Charlottown

looked well: led over 10 furlongs out:

weakened over 2 furlongs out

25 ran

1967
RIBOCCO
(Fulke Johnson Houghton)
22–1
second to Royal Palace, beaten 2½ lengths
brought wide turn into straight: headway 3
furlongs out: every chance 1 furlong out:
unable quicken
22 ran

1968
SIR IVOR
(Vincent O'Brien)
4–5 favourite
won by 1½ lengths from Connaught
has done well: looked well: steady headway
3 furlongs out: pulled out 1 furlong out:
quickened and led well inside final furlong:
easily
13 ran

1969
RIBOFILIO
(Fulke Johnson Houghton)
7–2 favourite
5th behind Blakeney
headway 5 furlongs out: every chance over 1
furlong out: ran on one pace
26 ran

1970
NIJINSKY
(Vincent O'Brien)
11–8 favourite
won by 2½ lengths from Gyr
looked well: 6th straight: shaken up 2

furlongs out: led 1 furlong out: comfortably
11 ran

1971
THE PARSON
(Noel Murless)
16–1
6th behind Mill Reef
looked well: headway final 2 furlongs: never
nearer
21 ran

1972
ROBERTO
(Vincent O'Brien)
3–1 favourite
won by a short head from Rheingold
held up: hampered 2 furlongs out:
squeezed through 1 furlong out: led close
home: all out
22 ran

1973
CAVO DORO
(Vincent O'Brien)
12–1
second to Morston, beaten half a length
looked well: steady headway 3 furlongs out:
every chance over 1 furlong out: edged left
final furlong: ran on well
25 ran

1974
ARTHURIAN
(Henry Cecil)
28–1

unplaced behind Snow Knight
[no comment in *Raceform*]
18 ran

1975
BRUNI
(Ryan Price)
16–1
unplaced behind Grundy
looked well: prominent 7 furlongs
18 ran

1976
EMPERY
(Maurice Zilber)
10–1
won by 3 lengths from Relkino
good sort: 4th straight: hard ridden 1½
furlongs out: led inside final furlong: ran
on well
23 ran

1977
THE MINSTREL
(Vincent O'Brien)
5–1
won by a neck from Hot Grove
looked well: good headway 6 furlongs out:
4th straight: hard ridden below distance: led
near finish: all out
22 ran

1978
INKERMAN
(Vincent O'Brien)
4–1 favourite

unplaced behind Shirley Heights
well grown: prominent till no extra
halfway
25 ran

1979
MILFORD
(Dick Hern)
15–2
unplaced behind Troy
looked well: 2nd straight: weakened 2
furlongs out
23 ran

1980
MONTEVERDI
(Vincent O'Brien)
8–1
unplaced behind Henbit
[no comment in *Raceform*]

1981
SHOTGUN
(Chris Thornton)
7–1
fourth behind Shergar, beaten 14 lengths
6th straight: hard ridden 3 furlongs out: ran
on one-paced
18 ran

1982
no ride

1983
TEENOSO
(Geoff Wragg)

231

9–2 favourite
won by 3 lengths from Carlingford
Castle
3rd straight: led over 3 furlongs out:
ran on well
21 ran

1984
ALPHABATIM
(Guy Harwood)
11–2
5th behind Secreto
looked well: pulled out 3 furlongs out: hard
ridden over 2 furlongs out: one pace
17 ran

1985
THEATRICAL
(Dermot Weld)
10–1
unplaced behind Slip Anchor
good sort: sixth straight: no headway final 3
furlongs
14 ran

1986–1990
no rides

1991
HOKUSAI
(Henry Cecil)

25–1
unplaced behind Generous
looked well: 4th straight: hard ridden 2
furlongs out: soon weakened
13 ran

1992
RODRIGO DE TRIANO
(Peter Chapple-Hyam)
13–2 favourite
unplaced behind Dr Devious
sweating: never nearer
18 ran

1993
FATHERLAND
(Vincent O'Brien)
8–1
unplaced behind Commander In Chief
workmanlike: scope: headway and 8th
straight: weakened over 2 furlongs out
16 ran

1994
KHAMASEEN
(John Dunlop)
33–1
5th behind Erhaab
2nd straight: ridden over 2 furlongs out: one
pace
25 ran

Summary

Rides	Wins	Second	Fourth
36	9	4	1

Lester's Other Derbys

It is a measure of the importance and influence of the Derby that the Epsom race has lent its name to similar contests all around the globe. Many of these are familiar to racing fans (Irish Derby, Kentucky Derby, and so on), while others are less so: for example, Pamplona II, dam of Lester's seventh Derby winner Empery, had won the Derby Nacional in her native Peru.

Lester has ridden in Derbys all around the world, and won several in addition to 'the' Derby at Epsom. These include:

IRISH DERBY (The Curragh)

1965	Meadow Court
1967	Ribocco
1968	Ribero
1977	The Minstrel
1981	Shergar

PRIX DU JOCKEY-CLUB (Longchamp – the French Derby)

1972	Hard To Beat

GERMAN DERBY (Hamburg)

1957	Orsini
1967	Luciano

ITALIAN DERBY (Rome)

1969	Bonconte di Monte Feltro
1973	Cerreto
1984	Welnor

ULSTER HARP DERBY (Down Royal)

1967	Dan Kano

SINGAPORE DERBY (Bukit Tima)
1979   Saas Fee

SWEDISH DERBY (Täby)
1958   Flying Friendship
1992   Tao

SLOVENSKE DERBY (Bratislava)
1993   Zimzalabim

Not forgetting, of course, the 'Pitmen's Derby' (the Northumberland Plate at Newcastle) on Little Cloud in 1955, and the Dockers' Derby at Manchester in 1957 on Dark Heron.

History does not record all Lester's performances in Donkey Derbys.

The Leading Derby Jockeys

LESTER PIGGOTT

9 wins

1954	Never Say Die
1957	Crepello
1960	St Paddy
1968	Sir Ivor
1970	Nijinsky
1972	Roberto
1976	Empery
1977	The Minstrel
1983	Teenoso

JEM ROBINSON

6 wins

1817	Azor
1824	Cedric
1825	Middleton
1827	Mameluke
1828	Cadland
1836	Bay Middleton

JOHN ARNULL

5 wins

1784	Sergeant
1790	Rhadamanthus
1796	Didelot
1799	Archduke
1807	Election

STEVE DONOGHUE

6 wins

1915	Pommern*
1917	Gay Crusader*
1921	Humorist
1922	Captain Cuttle
1923	Papyrus
1925	Manna

* wartime substitute race run at Newmarket

FRANK BUCKLE

5 wins

1792	John Bull
1794	Daedalus
1802	Tyrant
1811	Phantom
1823	Emilius

WILLIAM CLIFT

5 wins

1793	Waxy
1800	Champion
1803	Ditto
1810	Whalebone
1819	Tiresias

FRED ARCHER

5 wins

1877	Silvio
1880	Bend Or
1881	Iroquois
1885	Melton
1886	Ormonde

Winners four times have been Sam Arnull (1780 – the first running – to 1798), Tom Goodisson (1809 to 1822), Bill Scott (1832 to 1843), Jack Watts (1887 to 1896), Charlie Smirke (1934 to 1958) and Willie Carson (1979 to 1994).

Of jockeys with a licence at the start of the 2004 season, only three have won the Derby more than once:

MICHAEL KINANE

2 wins

1993 Commander In Chief

2001 Galileo

JOHNNY MURTAGH

2 wins

2000 Sinndar

2002 High Chaparral

KIEREN FALLON

2 wins

1999 Oath

2003 Kris Kin

Since the Derby returned to Epsom in 1946 after being run at Newmarket during the Second World War, the only jockeys apart from Lester to have ridden three or more Derby winners are Willie Carson (four) and Pat Eddery and Rae Johnstone (three each). (Charlie Smirke rode four in all, two before the war and two after.)

Lester's total of thirty-six Derby rides has been challenged since the war only by Pat Eddery with thirty-one, Joe Mercer (who never won the race) with thirty (in a single sequence between 1954 and 1983) and Willie Carson with twenty-eight.

Lester's Derby Winners
in Order of . . .

starting price

1968	SIR IVOR	4–5 favourite
1970	NIJINSKY	11–8 favourite
1957	CREPELLO	6–4 favourite
1972	ROBERTO	3–1 favourite
1983	TEENOSO	9–2 favourite
1977	THE MINSTREL	5–1
1960	ST PADDY	7–1
1976	EMPERY	10–1
1954	NEVER SAY DIE	33–1

winning distance

1972	ROBERTO	short head
1977	THE MINSTREL	neck
1957	CREPELLO	1½ lengths
1968	SIR IVOR	1½ lengths
1954	NEVER SAY DIE	2 lengths
1970	NIJINSKY	2½ lengths
1960	ST PADDY	3 lengths
1976	EMPERY	3 lengths
1983	TEENOSO	3 lengths

winning time

1970	NIJINSKY	2 mins 34.68 secs	(going: good)	
1957	CREPELLO	2 mins 35.4 secs	(firm)	
1960	ST PADDY	2 mins 35.6 secs	(firm)	*cont'd*

1976	EMPERY	2 mins 35.69 secs	(good)
1954	NEVER SAY DIE	2 mins 35.8 secs	(good)
1972	ROBERTO	2 mins 36.09 secs	(firm)
1977	THE MINSTREL	2 mins 36.44	(good)
1968	SIR IVOR	2 mins 38.7 secs	(good)
1983	TEENOSO	2 mins 49.07 secs	(heavy)

Timeform ratings (in pounds) at the end of
their three-year-old season

1970	NIJINSKY	138
1954	NEVER SAY DIE	137
1957	CREPELLO	136
1968	SIR IVOR	135
1977	THE MINSTREL	135
1960	ST PADDY	133
1983	TEENOSO	132
1972	ROBERTO	131
1976	EMPERY	128

winning trainers

4	VINCENT O'BRIEN (Sir Ivor, Nijinsky, Roberto, The Minstrel)
2	NOEL MURLESS (Crepello, St Paddy)
1	JOE LAWSON (Never Say Die)
1	MAURICE ZILBER (Empery)
1	GEOFF WRAGG (Teenoso)

The Derby Course

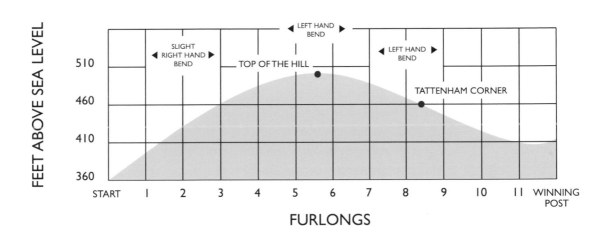

FEET ABOVE SEA LEVEL

510

460

410

360

START 1 2 3 4 5 6 7 8 9 10 11 WINNING POST

FURLONGS

SLIGHT RIGHT HAND BEND

TOP OF THE HILL

LEFT HAND BEND

LEFT HAND BEND

TATTENHAM CORNER

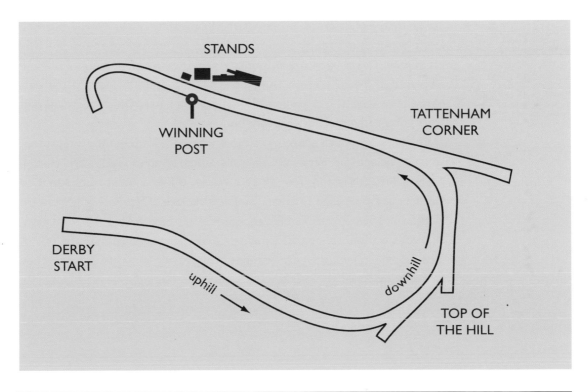

STANDS

WINNING POST

DERBY START

uphill

downhill

TATTENHAM CORNER

TOP OF THE HILL

Bibliography

Over the years there has not exactly been a world shortage of books about Lester Piggott. In addition to his own autobiography *Lester* (published in 1995), there have biographies by several authors, including Ivor Bailey, Claude Duval, Sean Pryor, James Lawton, John Karter, Julian Wilson, Roy David, Michael Tanner and Dick Francis – the last-named author having conducted extensive interviews with the man himself, and his book thereby enjoying an authority which some of the others lack.

The standard history of the Derby is *The History of the Derby Stakes* by Roger Mortimer, originally published in 1961, then republished in 1973 to conclude with Morston's victory by half a length from Lester on Cavo Doro. *The Epsom Derby* by Roger Mortimer with Tim Neligan, published in 1984, brought the story up to Secreto's last-gasp victory over El Gran Senor that year. There is an extensive bibliography of the Derby, but one less obvious text strongly recommended to enthusiasts of the race is the play *Epsom Downs* by Howard Brenton, published by Methuen in 1977 and discussed in the chapter on The Minstrel in the present book. To the best of my knowledge, it is the only work concerning Lester which observes that 'He's got an arse like a little cream bun.'

Other books which proved invaluable when putting together the present volume include Sir Peter O'Sullevan's autobiography *Calling the Horses*; *Thoroughbred Stallions* by Tony Morris; *Vincent O'Brien's Great Horses* by Ivor Herbert and Jacqueline O'Brien; *The Encyclopaedia of Flat Racing* by Howard Wright; and *The Guv'nor*, Tim Fitzgeorge-Parker's biography of Noel Murless.

It goes without saying that Timeform's *Racehorses* annuals and the official form book *Raceform*, the cornerstones of any racing library, have never been far from my side.

S.M.

Index

St Paddy 1960

Never say Die 1954

Empery 1976

Nijinsky 1970

Lester Piggott wins his fir